IN THE NAME OF PROFIT

Robert L. Heilbroner
Morton Mintz
Colman McCarthy
Sanford J. Ungar
Kermit Vandivier
Saul Friedman
James Boyd

IN THE NAME
OF PROFIT

DOUBLEDAY & COMPANY, INC.
Garden City, New York

CONTENTS

PART TWO

FOREWORD

Many books have reported the misdeeds of the American corporation—victimizing the consumer, exploiting the environment, and so on. This book, however, deals not with the baneful results of corporate irresponsibility but with its roots in human behavior. It tries to show what sort of men run the supercorporations, what their values are, and why they act as they do.

The book grew out of a conversation I had with Thomas Congdon, now Senior Editor at Doubleday. We felt that readers might understand corporate irresponsibility better if it were presented in terms of human beings rather than of economic institutions acting impersonally. Together we planned a book of "profiles," each of which would dig into one case of irresponsibility and show the key executive as he made his contemptible decision. The goal was to produce the first book that dramatized, through actual, named executives of major American companies, the sickness at the heart of the system.

To this end, six skilled investigative journalists were invited to look deeply into representative instances. Even for these experienced reporters, it was difficult to penetrate the corporate veil, and there is, for example, no instance of one of the most common kinds of corporate irresponsibility, the decision to pollute. Still, their chapters may succeed in casting the American executive in a new light. Though smoother and less openly rapacious than earlier generations of American entrepreneurs; though well-barbered and conservatively dressed; though fluent in lip service to the traditional virtues and emphatic about "responsibility" in his lectures to his sons and daughters, today's executive is often revealed here as a moral cripple, a man who has sold his soul to his employer, a man whose sense of social obligation is easily overwhelmed by his zeal for advancement and his rationalizations about the sanctity of profit. Indeed, the ease with which the executives in these chapters made their cynical choices—at the very first chance and without a qualm—suggests that they believed their behavior to be normal and acceptable within the world of the corporation, which in turn suggests that it is.

It is, of course, up to the reader to decide how representative these cases truly are. Our hope is merely that the chapters do, as Robert Heilbroner says in his own chapter of perspective, "serve to give life to questions that tend otherwise to become too abstract to command the thoughtful attention they require," and that they "make us ask . . . where responsibility begins and where it ends." So long as we continue to think of corporate irresponsibility in the old way, as a matter solely of economic institutions, not of individuals who are products of a system and a society, we can expect the corporation to continue to devour the substance and spirit of America, in the name of profit.

DAVID OBST

Washington, D.C.
October 1971

ABOUT THE AUTHORS

ROBERT L. HEILBRONER is known as one of the most readable of economists and social critics. His first book, *The Worldly Philosophers,* a celebrated history of economics, is a standard introduction to economics in many colleges and universities. Later books, including *The Future as History, The Great Ascent* and *Between Capitalism and Socialism,* have also reached wide academic and general audiences. Dr. Heilbroner is Norman Thomas Professor of Economics at the New School for Social Research in New York City.

COLMAN MCCARTHY is a reporter, essayist and editorial writer for the Washington *Post* and author of a forthcoming Houghton Mifflin book of profiles in social dissent. His series of *Post* articles revealing the dangerous condition of certain General Motors school buses—and GM's callous treatment of the bus owners—was credited with helping bring about the recall of 4200 GM school buses across the nation.

MORTON MINTZ is co-author of the best-selling book *America, Inc.,* and a reporter for the Washington *Post.* A former Nieman Fellow at Harvard, Mintz is the journalist who broke the story of the baby-deforming sedative thalidomide, an achievement that won him the Heywood Broun, the Raymond Clapper and the George Polk memorial awards.

SANFORD J. UNGAR is a graduate of Harvard and the London School of Economics. He worked for United Press International during the unrest in France in 1968 and co-authored a book describing that unrest, *The Almost Revolution.* Now a reporter for the Washington *Post,* he is author of the forthcoming Dutton book *The Papers and the Papers,* an account of the legal and political battle over the Pentagon Papers. Mr. Ungar wishes to thank Morton Mintz for assistance in preparing his chapter.

KERMIT VANDIVIER is a reporter for the Troy (Ohio) *Daily News,* and his assignments have included a tour in Vietnam. He first participated in and then exposed the business scandal he recounts in this book.

SAUL FRIEDMAN is Washington correspondent for the Knight Newspapers. He was a Nieman Fellow at Harvard and has been an investigative reporter since 1953.

JAMES BOYD is the executive director of the Fund for Investigative Journalism and a Contributing Editor of *The Washington Monthly.* In his book *Above the Law,* published in 1968, he told how, as administrative assistant to Senator Thomas Dodd, he helped lay bare the improprieties that led to Dodd's censure by his fellow senators. He is now at work on a novel with a Washington setting for W. W. Norton & Co.

DAVID OBST, who conceived and coordinated this book, was a founder of Reporters News Service, whose series revealing the My Lai massacres won a Pulitzer Prize in 1970. Mr. Obst studied Chinese at the University of California and did graduate work in Taipei. He is editor of *Ecotage* (Simon & Schuster) and of the forthcoming Doubleday book *A Television Viewer's Guide to the News*.

IN THE NAME OF PROFIT

PART ONE

CHAPTER ONE

"Why Should My Conscience Bother Me?"

by KERMIT VANDIVIER

THE B. F. Goodrich Co. is what business magazines like to speak of as "a major American corporation." It has operations in a dozen states and as many foreign countries, and of these far-flung facilities, the Goodrich plant at Troy, Ohio, is not the most imposing. It is a small, one-story building, once used to manufacture airplanes. Set in the grassy flatlands of west-central Ohio, it employs only about six hundred people. Nevertheless, it is one of the three largest manufacturers of aircraft wheels and brakes, a leader in a most profitable industry. Goodrich wheels and brakes support such well-known planes as the F111, the C5A, the Boeing 727, the XB70 and many others. Its customers include almost every aircraft manufacturer in the world.

Contracts for aircraft wheels and brakes often run into millions of dollars, and ordinarily a contract with a total value of less than $70,000, though welcome, would not create any special stir of joy in the hearts of Goodrich sales personnel. But purchase order P-23718, issued on June 18, 1967, by the LTV Aerospace Corporation, and ordering 202 brake assemblies for a new Air Force plane at a total price of $69,417, was received by Goodrich with considerable glee. And there was good reason. Some ten years previously, Goodrich had built a brake for LTV that was, to say the least, considerably less than a rousing success. The brake had not lived up to Goodrich's promises, and after experiencing considerable difficulty, LTV had written off Goodrich as a source of brakes. Since that time, Goodrich salesmen had been unable to sell so much as a shot of brake fluid to LTV. So in 1967, when LTV requested bids on wheels and brakes for the new A7D light attack aircraft it proposed to build for the Air Force, Goodrich submitted a bid that was absurdly low, so low that LTV could not, in all prudence, turn it down.

Goodrich had, in industry parlance, "bought into the business." Not only did the company not expect to make a profit on the deal; it was prepared, if necessary, to lose money. For aircraft brakes are not something that can be ordered off the shelf. They are designed for a particular aircraft, and once an aircraft manufacturer buys a brake, he is forced to purchase all replacement parts from the brake manufacturer. The $70,000 that Goodrich would get for making the brake would be a drop in the bucket when compared with the cost of the linings and other parts the Air Force would have to buy from Goodrich during the lifetime of the aircraft. Furthermore, the company which manufactures brakes for one particular model of an aircraft quite naturally has the inside track to supply other brakes when the planes are updated and improved.

Thus, that first contract, regardless of the money involved, is very important, and Goodrich, when it learned that it had been awarded the A7D contract, was determined that while it may have slammed the door on its own foot ten years before, this time, the second time around, things would be different. The word was soon circulated throughout the plant: "We can't bungle it this time. We've got to give them a good brake, regardless of the cost."

There was another factor which had undoubtedly influenced LTV. All aircraft brakes made today are of the disk type, and the bid submitted by Goodrich called for a relatively small brake, one containing four disks and weighing only 106 pounds. The weight of any aircraft part is extremely important. The lighter a part is, the heavier the plane's payload can be. The four-rotor, 106-pound brake promised by Goodrich was about as light as could be expected, and this undoubtedly had helped move LTV to award the contract to Goodrich.

The brake was designed by one of Goodrich's most capable engineers, John Warren. A tall, lanky blond and a graduate of Purdue, Warren had come from the Chrysler Corporation seven years before and had become adept at aircraft brake design. The happy-go-lucky manner he usually maintained belied a temper which exploded whenever anyone ventured to offer any criticism of his work, no matter how small. On these occasions, Warren would turn red in the face, often throwing or slamming something and then stalking from the scene. As his coworkers learned the consequences of criticizing him, they did so less and less readily, and when he submitted his preliminary design for the A7D brake, it was accepted without question.

Warren was named project engineer for the A7D, and he, in turn, assigned the task of producing the final production design to a newcomer to the Goodrich engineering stable, Searle Lawson. Just turned twenty-six, Lawson had been out of the Northrup Institute of Technology only one year when he came to Goodrich in January 1967. Like Warren, he had worked for a while in the automotive industry, but his engineering degree was in aeronautical and astronautical sciences, and when the opportunity came to enter his special field, via Goodrich, he took it. At the Troy plant, Lawson had been assigned to various "paper projects" to break him in, and after several months spent reviewing statistics and old brake designs, he was beginning to fret at the lack of challenge. When told he was being assigned to his first "real" project, he was elated and immediately plunged into his work.

The major portion of the design had already been completed by Warren, and major assemblies for the brake had already been ordered from Goodrich suppliers. Naturally, however, before Goodrich could start making the brakes on a production basis, much testing would have to be done. Lawson would have to determine the best materials to use for the linings and discover what minor adjustments in the design would have to be made.

Then, after the preliminary testing and after the brake was judged ready for production, one whole brake assembly would undergo a series of grueling, simulated braking stops and other severe trials called qualification tests. These tests are required by the military, which gives very detailed specifications on how they are to be conducted, the criteria for failure, and so on. They are performed in the Goodrich plant's test laboratory, where huge machines called dynamometers can simulate the weight and speed of almost any aircraft. After the brakes pass the laboratory tests, they are approved for production, but before the brakes are accepted for use in military service, they must undergo further extensive flight tests.

Searle Lawson was well aware that much work had to be done before the A7D brake could go into production, and he knew that LTV had set the last two weeks in June, 1968, as the starting dates for flight tests. So he decided to begin testing immediately. Goodrich's suppliers had not yet delivered the brake housing and other parts, but the brake disks had arrived, and using the housing from a brake similar in size and weight to the A7D brake, Lawson built a prototype. The prototype was installed in a test wheel and placed on one of the big dynamometers in the plant's test laboratory. The dynamometer was adjusted to simulate the weight of the A7D and Lawson began a series of tests, "landing" the wheel and brake at the A7D's landing speed, and braking it to a stop. The main purpose of these preliminary tests was to learn what temperatures would develop within the brake during the simulated stops and to evaluate the lining materials tentatively selected for use.

During a normal aircraft landing the temperatures inside the brake may reach 1000 degrees, and occasionally a bit higher. During Lawson's first simulated landings, the temperature of his prototype brake reached 1500 degrees. The

brake glowed a bright cherry-red and threw off incandes-
cent particles of metal and lining material as the temperature reached its peak. After a few such stops, the brake
was dismantled and the linings were found to be almost
completely disintegrated. Lawson chalked this first failure
up to chance and, ordering new lining materials, tried
again.

The second attempt was a repeat of the first. The brake
became extremely hot, causing the lining materials to
crumble into dust.

After the third such failure, Lawson, inexperienced
though he was, knew that the fault lay not in defective
parts or unsuitable lining material but in the basic design
of the brake itself. Ignoring Warren's original computations, Lawson made his own, and it didn't take him long
to discover where the trouble lay—the brake was too
small. There simply was not enough surface area on the
disks to stop the aircraft without generating the excessive
heat that caused the linings to fail.

The answer to the problem was obvious but far from
simple—the four-disk brake would have to be scrapped,
and a new design, using five disks, would have to be
developed. The implications were not lost on Lawson.
Such a step would require the junking of all the four-
disk-brake subassemblies, many of which had now begun
to arrive from the various suppliers. It would also mean
several weeks of preliminary design and testing and many
more weeks of waiting while the suppliers made and delivered the new subassemblies.

Yet, several weeks had already gone by since LTV's
order had arrived, and the date for delivery of the first
production brakes for flight testing was only a few months
away.

Although project engineer John Warren had more or less turned the A7D over to Lawson, he knew of the difficulties Lawson had been experiencing. He had assured the young engineer that the problem revolved around getting the right kind of lining material. Once that was found, he said, the difficulties would end.

Despite the evidence of the abortive tests and Lawson's careful computations, Warren rejected the suggestion that the four-disk brake was too light for the job. Warren knew that his superior had already told LTV, in rather glowing terms, that the preliminary tests on the A7D brake were very successful. Indeed, Warren's superiors weren't aware at this time of the troubles on the brake. It would have been difficult for Warren to admit not only that he had made a serious error in his calculations and original design but that his mistakes had been caught by a green kid, barely out of college.

Warren's reaction to a five-disk brake was not unexpected by Lawson, and, seeing that the four-disk brake was not to be abandoned so easily, he took his calculations and dismal test results one step up the corporate ladder.

At Goodrich, the man who supervises the engineers working on projects slated for production is called, predictably, the projects manager. The job was held by a short, chubby and bald man named Robert Sink. A man truly devoted to his work, Sink was as likely to be found at his desk at ten o'clock on Sunday night as ten o'clock on Monday morning. His outside interests consisted mainly of tinkering on a Model-A Ford and an occasional game of golf. Some fifteen years before, Sink had begun working at Goodrich as a lowly draftsman. Slowly, he worked his way up. Despite his geniality, Sink was neither respected nor liked by the majority of the engineers, and his appointment as their supervisor did not improve their feelings about him. They thought he had only gone to high school. It quite naturally rankled those who had gone through years of college and acquired impressive specialties such as thermodynamics and astronautics to be commanded by a man whom they considered their intellectual inferior. But, though Sink had no college training, he had something even more useful: a fine working knowledge of company politics.

Puffing upon a Meerschaum pipe, Sink listened gravely as young Lawson confided his fears about the four-disk brake. Then he examined Lawson's calculations and the results of the abortive tests. Despite the fact that he was not a qualified engineer, in the strictest sense of the word, it must certainly have been obvious to Sink that Lawson's calculations were correct and that a four-disk brake would never have worked on the A7D.

But other things of equal importance were also obvious. First, to concede that Lawson's calculations were correct would also mean conceding that Warren's calculations were incorrect. As projects manager, he not only was responsible for Warren's activities, but, in admitting that Warren had erred, he would have to admit that he had erred in trusting Warren's judgment. It also meant that, as projects manager, it would be he who would have to explain the whole messy situation to the Goodrich hierarchy, not only at Troy but possibly on the corporate level at Goodrich's Akron offices. And, having taken Warren's judgment of the four-disk brake at face value (he was forced to do this since, not being an engineer, he was unable to exercise any engineering judgment of his own), he had assured LTV, not once but several times, that about all there was left to do on the brake was pack it in a crate and ship it out the back door.

There's really no problem at all, he told Lawson. After all, Warren was an experienced engineer, and if he said the brake would work, it would work. Just keep on testing and probably, maybe even on the very next try, it'll work out just fine.

Lawson was far from convinced, but without the support of his superiors there was little he could do except keep on testing. By now, housings for the four-disk brake had begun to arrive at the plant, and Lawson was able to build up a production model of the brake and begin the formal qualification tests demanded by the military.

The first qualification attempts went exactly as the tests on the prototype had. Terrific heat developed within the brakes and, after a few, short, simulated stops, the linings crumbled. A new type of lining material was ordered and once again an attempt to qualify the brake was made. Again, failure.

Experts were called in from lining manufacturers, and new lining "mixes" were tried, always with the same result. Failure.

It was now the last week in March 1968, and flight tests were scheduled to begin in seventy days. Twelve separate attempts had been made to formally qualify the brake, and all had failed. It was no longer possible for anyone to ignore the glaring truth that the brake was a dismal failure and that nothing short of a major design change could ever make it work.

In the engineering department, panic set in. A glum-faced Lawson prowled the test laboratory dejectedly. Occasionally, Warren would witness some simulated stop on the brake and, after it was completed, troop silently back to his desk. Sink, too, showed an unusual interest in the trials, and he and Warren would converse in low tones while poring over the results of the latest tests. Even the most inexperienced of the lab technicians and the men who operated the testing equipment knew they had a "bad" brake on their hands, and there was some grumbling about "wasting time on a brake that won't work."

New menaces appeared. An engineering team from LTV arrived at the plant to get a good look at the brake in action. Luckily, they stayed only a few days, and Goodrich engineers managed to cover the true situation without too much difficulty.

On April 4, the thirteenth attempt at qualification was begun. This time no attempt was made to conduct the tests by the methods and techniques spelled out in the military specifications. Regardless of how it had to be done, the brake was to be "nursed" through the required fifty simulated stops.

Fans were set up to provide special cooling. Instead of maintaining pressure on the brake until the test wheel had come to a complete stop, the pressure was reduced when the wheel had decelerated to around 15 mph, allowing it to "coast" to a stop. After each stop, the brake was disassembled and carefully cleaned, and after some of the stops, internal brake parts were machined in order to remove warp and other disfigurations caused by the high heat.

By these and other methods, all clearly contrary to the techniques established by the military specifications, the brake was coaxed through the fifty stops. But even using these methods, the brake could not meet all the require-

ments. On one stop the wheel rolled for a distance of
16,000 feet, nearly three miles, before the brake could
bring it to a stop. The normal distance required for such
a stop was around 3500 feet.

On April 11, the day the thirteenth test was completed,
I became personally involved in the A7D situation.

I had worked in the Goodrich test laboratory for five
years, starting first as an instrumentation engineer, then
later becoming a data analyst and technical writer. As
part of my duties, I analyzed the reams and reams of instrumentation data that came from the many testing machines in the laboratory, then transcribed it to a more
usable form for the engineering department. And when a
new-type brake had successfully completed the required
qualification tests, I would issue a formal qualification report.

Qualification reports were an accumulation of all the
data and test logs compiled by the test technicians during
the qualification tests, and were documentary proof that
a brake had met all the requirements established by the
military specifications and was therefore presumed safe
for flight testing. Before actual flight tests were conducted on a brake, qualification reports had to be delivered to the customer and to various government officials.

On April 11, I was looking over the data from the
latest A7D test, and I noticed that many irregularities in
testing methods had been noted on the test logs.

Technically, of course, there was nothing wrong with
conducting tests in any manner desired, so long as the
test was for research purposes only. But qualification test
methods are clearly delineated by the military, and I

knew that this test had been a formal qualification attempt. One particular notation on the test logs caught my eye. For some of the stops, the instrument which recorded the brake pressure had been deliberately miscalibrated so that, while the brake pressure used during the stops was recorded as 1000 psi (the maximum pressure that would be available on the A7D aircraft), the pressure had actually been 1100 psi!

I showed the test logs to the test lab supervisor, Ralph Gretzinger, who said he had learned from the technician who had miscalibrated the instrument that he had been asked to do so by Lawson. Lawson, said Gretzinger, readily admitted asking for the miscalibration, saying he had been told to do so by Sink.

I asked Gretzinger why anyone would want to miscalibrate the data-recording instruments.

"Why? I'll tell you why," he snorted. "That brake is a failure. It's way too small for the job, and they're not ever going to get it to work. They're getting desperate, and instead of scrapping the damned thing and starting over, they figure they can horse around down here in the lab and qualify it that way."

An expert engineer, Gretzinger had been responsible for several innovations in brake design. It was he who had invented the unique brake system used on the famous XB70. A graduate of Georgia Tech, he was a stickler for detail and he had some very firm ideas about honesty and ethics. "If you want to find out what's going on," said Gretzinger, "ask Lawson, he'll tell you."

Curious, I did ask Lawson the next time he came into the lab. He seemed eager to discuss the A7D and gave me the history of his months of frustrating efforts to get

Warren and Sink to change the brake design. "I just can't believe this is really happening," said Lawson, shaking his head slowly. "This isn't engineering, at least not what I thought it would be. Back in school, I thought that when you were an engineer, you tried to do your best, no matter what it cost. But this is something else."

He sat across the desk from me, his chin propped in his hand. "Just wait," he warned. "You'll get a chance to see what I'm talking about. You're going to get in the act, too, because I've already had the word that we're going to make one more attempt to qualify the brake, and that's it. Win or lose, we're going to issue a qualification report!"

I reminded him that a qualification report could only be issued after a brake had successfully met all military requirements, and therefore, unless the next qualification attempt was a success, no report would be issued.

"You'll find out," retorted Lawson. "I was already told that regardless of what the brake does on test, it's going to be qualified." He said he had been told in those exact words at a conference with Sink and Russell Van Horn.

This was the first indication that Sink had brought his boss, Van Horn, into the mess. Although Van Horn, as manager of the design engineering section, was responsible for the entire department, he was not necessarily familiar with all phases of every project, and it was not uncommon for those under him to exercise the what-he-doesn't-know-won't-hurt-him philosophy. If he was aware of the full extent of the A7D situation, it meant that matters had truly reached a desperate stage—that Sink had decided not only to call for help but was looking toward that moment when blame must be borne and, if possible, shared.

Also, if Van Horn had said, "regardless what the brake does on test, it's going to be qualified," then it could only mean that, if necessary, a false qualification report would be issued! I discussed this possibility with Gretzinger, and he assured me that under no circumstances would such a report ever be issued.

"If they want a qualification report, we'll write them one, but we'll tell it just like it is," he declared emphatically. "No false data or false reports are going to come out of this lab."

On May 2, 1968, the fourteenth and final attempt to qualify the brake was begun. Although the same improper methods used to nurse the brake through the previous tests were employed, it soon became obvious that this too would end in failure.

When the tests were about half completed, Lawson asked if I would start preparing the various engineering curves and graphic displays which were normally incorporated in a qualification report. "It looks as though you'll be writing a qualification report shortly," he said.

I flatly refused to have anything to do with the matter and immediately told Gretzinger what I had been asked to do. He was furious and repeated his previous declaration that under no circumstances would any false data or other matter be issued from the lab.

"I'm going to get this settled right now, once and for all," he declared. "I'm going to see Line [Russell Line, manager of the Goodrich Technical Services Section, of which the test lab was a part] and find out just how far this thing is going to go!" He stormed out of the room.

In about an hour, he returned and called me to his desk. He sat silently for a few moments, then muttered, half to himself, "I wonder what the hell they'd do if I just quit?" I didn't answer and I didn't ask him what he meant. I knew. He had been beaten down. He had reached the point when the decision had to be made. Defy them now while there was still time—or knuckle under, sell out.

"You know," he went on uncertainly, looking down at his desk, "I've been an engineer for a long time, and I've always believed that ethics and integrity were every bit as important as theorems and formulas, and never once has anything happened to change my beliefs. Now this . . . Hell, I've got two sons I've got to put through school and I just . . ." His voice trailed off.

He sat for a few more minutes, then, looking over the top of his glasses, said hoarsely, "Well, it looks like we're licked. The way it stands now, we're to go ahead and prepare the data and other things for the graphic presentation in the report, and when we're finished, someone upstairs will actually write the report.

"After all," he continued, "we're just drawing some curves, and what happens to them after they leave here, well, we're not responsible for that."

He was trying to persuade himself that as long as we were concerned with only one part of the puzzle and didn't see the completed picture, we really weren't doing anything wrong. He didn't believe what he was saying, and he knew I didn't believe it either. It was an embarrassing and shameful moment for both of us.

I wasn't at all satisfied with the situation and decided that I too would discuss the matter with Russell Line, the senior executive in our section.

Tall, powerfully built, his teeth flashing white, his face

tanned to a coffee-brown by a daily stint with a sun lamp, Line looked and acted every inch the executive. He was a crossword-puzzle enthusiast and an ardent golfer, and though he had lived in Troy only a short time, he had been accepted into the Troy Country Club and made an official of the golf committee. He had been transferred from the Akron offices some two years previously, and an air of mystery surrounded him. Some office gossips figured he had been sent to Troy as the result of some sort of demotion. Others speculated that since the present general manager of the Troy plant was due shortly for retirement, Line had been transferred to Troy to assume that job and was merely occupying his present position to "get the feel of things." Whatever the case, he commanded great respect and had come to be well liked by those of us who worked under him.

He listened sympathetically while I explained how I felt about the A7D situation, and when I had finished, he asked me what I wanted him to do about it. I said that as employees of the Goodrich Company we had a responsibility to protect the company and its reputation if at all possible. I said I was certain that officers on the corporate level would never knowingly allow such tactics as had been employed on the A7D.

"I agree with you," he remarked, "but I still want to know what you want me to do about it."

I suggested that in all probability the chief engineer at the Troy plant, H. C. "Bud" Sunderman, was unaware of the A7D problem and that he, Line, should tell him what was going on.

Line laughed, good-humoredly. "Sure, I could, but I'm not going to. Bud probably already knows about this thing anyway, and if he doesn't, I'm sure not going to be the one to tell him."

"But why?"

"Because it's none of my business, and it's none of yours. I learned a long time ago not to worry about things over which I had no control. I have no control over this."

I wasn't satisfied with this answer, and I asked him if his conscience wouldn't bother him if, say, during flight tests on the brake, something should happen resulting in death or injury to the test pilot.

"Look," he said, becoming somewhat exasperated, "I just told you I have no control over this thing. Why should my conscience bother me?"

His voice took on a quiet, soothing tone as he continued. "You're just getting all upset over this thing for nothing. I just do as I'm told, and I'd advise you to do the same."

He had made his decision, and now I had to make mine.

I made no attempt to rationalize what I had been asked to do. It made no difference who would falsify which part of the report or whether the actual falsification would be by misleading numbers or misleading words. Whether by acts of commission or omission, all of us who contributed to the fraud would be guilty. The only question left for me to decide was whether or not I would become a party to the fraud.

Before coming to Goodrich in 1963, I had held a variety of jobs, each a little more pleasant, a little more rewarding than the last. At forty-two, with seven children, I had decided that the Goodrich Company would probably

be my "home" for the rest of my working life. The job
paid well, it was pleasant and challenging, and the future
looked reasonably bright. My wife and I had bought a
home and we were ready to settle down into a comfortable,
middle-age, middle-class rut. If I refused to take part
in the A7D fraud, I would have to either resign or be fired.
The report would be written by someone anyway, but I
would have the satisfaction of knowing I had had no part
in the matter. But bills aren't paid with personal satisfaction, nor house payments with ethical principles. I made
my decision. The next morning, I telephoned Lawson and
told him I was ready to begin on the qualification report.

In a few minutes, he was at my desk, ready to begin.
Before we started, I asked him, "Do you realize what we
are going to do?"

"Yeah," he replied bitterly, "we're going to screw LTV.
And speaking of screwing," he continued, "I know now
how a whore feels, because that's exactly what I've become, an engineering whore. I've sold myself. It's all I can
do to look at myself in the mirror when I shave. I make
me sick."

I was surprised at his vehemence. It was obvious that
he too had done his share of soul-searching and didn't
like what he had found. Somehow, though, the air seemed
clearer after his outburst, and we began working on the
report.

I had written dozens of qualification reports, and I
knew what a "good" one looked like. Resorting to the
actual test data only on occasion, Lawson and I proceeded to prepare page after page of elaborate, detailed engineering curves, charts, and test logs, which purported to show what had happened during the formal

qualification tests. Where temperatures were too high, we deliberately chopped them down a few hundred degrees, and where they were too low, we raised them to a value that would appear reasonable to the LTV and military engineers. Brake pressure, torque values, distances, times— everything of consequence was tailored to fit the occasion.

Occasionally, we would find that some test either hadn't been performed at all or had been conducted improperly. On those occasions, we "conducted" the test—successfully, of course—on paper.

For nearly a month we worked on the graphic presentation that would be a part of the report. Meanwhile, the fourteenth and final qualification attempt had been completed, and the brake, not unexpectedly, had failed again.

During that month, Lawson and I talked of little else except the enormity of what we were doing. The more involved we became in our work, the more apparent became our own culpability. We discussed such things as the Nuremberg trials and how they related to our guilt and complicity in the A7D situation. Lawson often expressed his opinion that the brake was downright dangerous and that, once on flight tests, "anything is liable to happen."

I saw his boss, John Warren, at least twice during that month and needled him about what we were doing. He didn't take the jibes too kindly but managed to laugh the situation off as "one of those things." One day I remarked that what we were doing amounted to fraud, and he pulled out an engineering handbook and turned to a section on laws as they related to the engineering profession.

He read the definition of fraud aloud, then said, "Well, technically I don't think what we're doing can be called fraud. I'll admit it's not right, but it's just one of those things. We're just kinda caught in the middle. About all I can tell you is, Do like I'm doing. Make copies of everything and put them in your SYA file."

"What's an 'SYA' file?" I asked.

"That's a 'save your ass' file." He laughed.

Although I hadn't known it was called that, I had been keeping an SYA file since the beginning of the A7D fiasco. I had made a copy of every scrap of paper connected even remotely with the A7D and had even had copies of 16mm movies that had been made during some of the simulated stops. Lawson, too, had an SYA file, and we both maintained them for one reason: Should the true state of events on the A7D ever be questioned, we wanted to have access to a complete set of factual data. We were afraid that should the question ever come up, the test data might accidentally be "lost."

We finished our work on the graphic portion of the report around the first of June. Altogether, we had prepared nearly two hundred pages of data, containing dozens of deliberate falsifications and misrepresentations. I delivered the data to Gretzinger, who said he had been instructed to deliver it personally to the chief engineer, Bud Sunderman, who in turn would assign someone in the engineering department to complete the written portion of the report. He gathered the bundle of data and left the office. Within minutes, he was back with the data, his face white with anger.

"That damned Sink's beat me to it," he said furiously. "He's already talked to Bud about this, and now Sunderman says no one in the engineering department has time to write the report. He wants us to do it, and I told him we couldn't."

The words had barely left his mouth when Russell Line burst in the door. "What the hell's all the fuss about this damned report?" he demanded loudly.

Patiently, Gretzinger explained. "There's no fuss. Sunderman just told me that we'd have to write the report down here, and I said we couldn't. Russ," he went on, "I've told you before that we weren't going to write the report. I made my position clear on that a long time ago."

Line shut him up with a wave of his hand and, turning to me, bellowed, "I'm getting sick and tired of hearing about this damned report. Now, write the goddam thing and shut up about it!" He slammed out of the office.

Gretzinger and I just sat for a few seconds looking at each other. Then he spoke.

"Well, I guess he's made it pretty clear, hasn't he? We can either write the thing or quit. You know, what we should have done was quit a long time ago. Now, it's too late."

Somehow, I wasn't at all surprised at this turn of events, and it didn't really make that much difference. As far as I was concerned, we were all up to our necks in the thing anyway, and writing the narrative portion of the report couldn't make me any more guilty than I already felt myself to be.

Still, Line's order came as something of a shock. All the time Lawson and I were working on the report, I felt, deep down, that somewhere, somehow, something would come along and the whole thing would blow over. But Russell Line had crushed that hope. The report was actually going to be issued. Intelligent, law-abiding officials of B. F. Goodrich, one of the oldest and most respected of American corporations, were actually going to deliver to a customer a product that was known to be defective and dangerous and which could very possibly cause death or serious injury.

Within two days, I had completed the narrative, or written portion of the report. As a final sop to my own self-respect, in the conclusion of the report I wrote, "The B. F. Goodrich P/N 2-1162-3 brake assembly does not meet the intent or the requirements of the applicable specification documents and therefore is not qualified."

This was a meaningless gesture, since I knew that this would certainly be changed when the report went through the final typing process. Sure enough, when the report was published, the negative conclusion had been made positive.

One final and significant incident occurred just before publication.

Qualification reports always bear the signature of the person who has prepared them. I refused to sign the report, as did Lawson. Warren was later asked to sign the report. He replied that he would "when I receive a signed statement from Bob Sink ordering me to sign it."

The engineering secretary who was delegated the responsibility of "dogging" the report through publication, told me later that after I, Lawson, and Warren had all refused to sign the report, she had asked Sink if he would sign. He replied, "On something of this nature, I don't think a signature is really needed."

On June 5, 1968, the report was officially published and copies were delivered in person to the Air Force and LTV. Within a week, flight tests were begun at Edwards Air Force Base in California. Searle Lawson was sent to California as Goodrich's representative. Within approximately two weeks, he returned because some rather unusual incidents during the tests had caused them to be canceled.

His face was grim as he related stories of several near crashes during landings—caused by brake troubles. He told me about one incident in which, upon landing, one brake was literally welded together by the intense heat developed during the test stop. The wheel locked, and the plane skidded for nearly 1500 feet before coming to a halt. The plane was jacked up and the wheel removed. The fused parts within the brake had to be pried apart.

Lawson had returned to Troy from California that same day, and that evening, he and others of the Goodrich engineering department left for Dallas for a high-level conference with LTV.

That evening I left work early and went to see my attorney. After I told him the story, he advised that, while I was probably not actually guilty of fraud, I was certainly part of a conspiracy to defraud. He advised me to go to the Federal Bureau of Investigation and offered to arrange an appointment. The following week he took me to the Dayton office of the FBI, and after I had been warned that I would not be immune from prosecution, I disclosed the A7D matter to one of the agents. The agent told me to say nothing about the episode to anyone and to report any further incident to him. He said he would forward the story to his superiors in Washington.

A few days later, Lawson returned from the conference in Dallas and said that the Air Force, which had previously approved the qualification report, had suddenly rescinded that approval and was demanding to see some of the raw test data taken during the tests. I gathered that the FBI had passed the word.

Omitting any reference to the FBI, I told Lawson I had been to an attorney and that we were probably guilty of conspiracy.

"Can you get me an appointment with your attorney?" he asked. Within a week, he had been to the FBI and told them of his part in the mess. He too was advised to say nothing but to keep on the job reporting any new development.

Naturally, with the rescinding of Air Force approval and the demand to see raw test data, Goodrich officials were in a panic. A conference was called for July 27, a Saturday morning affair at which Lawson, Sink, Warren and myself were present. We met in a tiny conference room in the deserted engineering department. Lawson and I, by now openly hostile to Warren and Sink, ranged ourselves on one side of the conference table while Warren sat on the other side. Sink, chairing the meeting, paced slowly in front of a blackboard, puffing furiously on a pipe.

The meeting was called, Sink began, "to see where we stand on the A7D." What we were going to do, he said, was to "level" with LTV and tell them the "whole truth" about the A7D. "After all," he said, "they're in this thing with us, and they have the right to know how matters stand."

"In other words," I asked, "we're going to tell them the truth?"

"That's right," he replied. "We're going to level with them and let them handle the ball from there."

"There's one thing I don't quite understand," I interjected. "Isn't it going to be pretty hard for us to admit to them that we've lied?"

"Now, wait a minute," he said angrily. "Let's don't go off half-cocked on this thing. It's not a matter of lying. We've just interpreted the information the way we felt it should be."

"I don't know what you call it," I replied, "but to me it's lying, and it's going to be damned hard to confess to them that we've been lying all along."

He became very agitated at this and repeated his "We're not lying," adding, "I don't like this sort of talk."

I dropped the matter at this point, and he began discussing the various discrepancies in the report.

We broke for lunch, and afterward, I came back to the plant to find Sink sitting alone at his desk, waiting to resume the meeting. He called me over and said he wanted to apologize for his outburst that morning. "This thing has kind of gotten me down," he confessed, "and I think you've got the wrong picture. I don't think you really understand everything about this."

Perhaps so, I conceded, but it seemed to me that if we had already told LTV one thing and then had to tell them another, changing our story completely, we would have to admit we were lying.

"No," he explained patiently, "we're not really lying. All we were doing was interpreting the figures the way we knew they should be. We were just exercising engineering license."

During the afternoon session, we marked some forty-three discrepant points in the report: forty-three points that LTV would surely spot as occasions where we had exercised "engineering license."

After Sink listed those points on the blackboard, we discussed each one individually. As each point came up,

Sink would explain that it was probably "too minor to bother about," or that perhaps it "wouldn't be wise to open that can of worms," or that maybe this was a point that "LTV just wouldn't understand." When the meeting was over, it had been decided that only three points were "worth mentioning."

Similar conferences were held during August and September, and the summer was punctuated with frequent treks between Dallas and Troy, and demands by the Air Force to see the raw test data. Tempers were short and matters seemed to grow worse.

Finally, early in October 1968, Lawson submitted his resignation, to take effect on October 25. On October 18, I submitted my own resignation, to take effect on November 1. In my resignation, addressed to Russell Line, I cited the A7D report and stated: "As you are aware, this report contained numerous deliberate and willful misrepresentations which, according to legal counsel, constitute fraud and expose both myself and others to criminal charges of conspiracy to defraud . . . The events of the past seven months have created an atmosphere of deceit and distrust in which it is impossible to work . . ."

On October 25, I received a sharp summons to the office of Bud Sunderman. As chief engineer at the Troy plant, Sunderman was responsible for the entire engineering division. Tall and graying, impeccably dressed at all times, he was capable of producing a dazzling smile or a hearty chuckle or immoblizing his face into marble hardness, as the occasion required.

I faced the marble hardness when I reached his office. He motioned me to a chair. "I have your resignation here," he snapped, "and I must say you have made some rather shocking, I might even say irresponsible, charges. This is very serious."

Before I could reply, he was demanding an explanation. "I want to know exactly what the fraud is in connection with the A7D and how you can dare accuse this company of such a thing!"

I started to tell some of the things that had happened during the testing, but he shut me off saying, "There's nothing wrong with anything we've done here. You aren't aware of all the things that have been going on behind the scenes. If you had known the true situation, you would never have made these charges." He said that in view of my apparent "disloyalty" he had decided to accept my resignation "right now," and said it would be better for all concerned if I left the plant immediately. As I got up to leave he asked me if I intended to "carry this thing further."

I answered simply, "Yes," to which he replied, "Suit yourself." Within twenty minutes, I had cleaned out my desk and left. Forty-eight hours later, the B. F. Goodrich Company recalled the qualification report and the four-disk brake, announcing that it would replace the brake with a new, improved, five-disk brake at no cost to LTV.

Ten months later, on August 13, 1969, I was the chief government witness at a hearing conducted before Senator William Proxmire's Economy in Government Subcommittee of the Congress's Joint Economic Committee. I related the A7D story to the committee, and my testimony was supported by Searle Lawson, who followed me to the witness stand. Air Force officers also testified, as well as a four-man team from the General Accounting Office, which had conducted an investigation of the A7D brake at the request of Senator Proxmire. Both Air Force and GAO investigators declared that the brake was dangerous and had not been tested properly.

Testifying for Goodrich was R. G. Jeter, vice-president and general counsel of the company, from the Akron headquarters. Representing the Troy plant was Robert Sink. These two denied any wrongdoing on the part of the Goodrich Company, despite expert testimony to the contrary by Air Force and GAO officials. Sink was quick to deny any connection with the writing of the report or of directing any falsifications, claiming to be on the West Coast at the time. John Warren was the man who supervised its writing, said Sink.

As for me, I was dismissed as a high-school graduate with no technical training, while Sink testified that Lawson was a young, inexperienced engineer. "We tried to give him guidance," Sink testified, "but he preferred to have his own convictions."

About changing the data and figures in the report, Sink said: "When you take data from several different sources, you have to rationalize among those data what is the true story. This is part of your engineering know-how." He admitted that changes had been made in the data, "but only to make them more consistent with the over-all picture of the data that is available."

Jeter pooh-poohed the suggestion that anything improper occurred, saying: "We have thirty-odd engineers at this plant . . . and I say to you that it is incredible that these men would stand idly by and see reports changed or falsified. . . . I mean you just do not have to do that working for anybody. . . . Just nobody does that."

The four-hour hearing adjourned with no real conclusion

reached by the committee. But, the following day the Department of Defense made sweeping changes in its inspection, testing and reporting procedures. A spokesman for the DOD said the changes were a result of the Goodrich episode.

The A7D is now in service, sporting a Goodrich-made five-disk brake, a brake that works very well, I'm told. Business at the Goodrich plant is good. Lawson is now an engineer for LTV and has been assigned to the A7D project. And I am now a newspaper reporter.

At this writing, those remaining at Goodrich are still secure in the same positions, all except Russell Line and Robert Sink. Line has been rewarded with a promotion to production superintendent, a large step upward on the corporate ladder. As for Sink, he moved up into Line's old job.

CHAPTER TWO

Deciding To Cheapen the Product

by COLMAN McCARTHY

T HE capital of American political power is Washington, D.C., but for those who regard money as more formidable than laws, the real power is elsewhere—in Detroit. In the board rooms of General Motors—the world's mightiest corporation, with 55 percent of the United States automobile market—decisions are routinely made that affect the lives of Americans in ways that the actions of Congressmen seldom do. By the hard measure of dollars, little doubt exists about the comparative importance between Detroit and Washington. At a recent peak year, 1969, the board chairman of General Motors was paid $655,000, or fifteen times the salary of a United States

Senator and more than three times what Americans pay their President. General Motors has an annual budget based on $24 billion in gross annual sales (1969 figures), a sum larger than the budget of any of the fifty states and every world nation except the United States and the Soviet Union.

One reason for the corporation's gargantuan size is that its customers keep coming back to buy its products, especially its cars, trucks and buses available at some 13,000 GM dealerships. Many return because they have been trained to crave the chrome, horsepower and gizmos that GM puts into its vehicles. Other consumers have a different reason for returning very frequently to the automotive market which GM dominates. These are the trapped victims of a corporate philosophy candidly described in April 1970 by then the board chairman James M. Roche, and a 42-year veteran of GM: "Planned obsolescence in my opinion is another word for progress."

Those words may seem mild, even reasonable. For this is a time when euphemism has all but vanquished the critical ear. Why needlessly attach harsh words to harsh acts when gentle words are available? Thus, when the expression "planned obsolescence . . . is another word for progress" is translated into plain language, the words seem mild. But the meaning is clear: "Go cheapen the product so we can make more money." And the underlings in the auto industry easily divine the true intentions of their superiors. They go cheapen the product, and GM makes more money. Quite a lot of money. According to GM's own records, their cumulative profit from 1947 to 1969 was $22 billion.

Only in recent years have numbers of Americans become concerned about the human cost of this policy of planned obsolescence—its impact on the lives of the people who ride in GM vehicles and the innocent people near those vehicles. In February 1969, for example, GM was obliged to notify 5.4 million owners to bring in their GM vehicles for correction of possible safety defects. Out of these, some 2.5 million were recalled to be checked for exhaust-system leaks. According to the Center for Auto Safety, these leaks were acknowledged by GM to have caused four deaths. How many other deaths were caused by the defect is unknown. Three months later, GM was obliged to warn owners of 1960–65 three-quarter-ton trucks that the vehicles were built in such a way that they did not function properly when overloaded. This was news to some owners, but not all; the National Highway Safety Bureau knew of at least twenty injuries in accidents caused by the splitting of wheel disks on the trucks.

It is unlikely that GM chairman James Roche ever sends out memos to his staff saying things like, "Make the exhaust systems out of cheaper metal this year," or "Order a lower-grade iron for the wheel disks on those three-quarter-ton trucks." Yet in many such cases he might as well. GM has had to call back millions of relatively new cars, and one may assume that countless others have defects which go unrectified. (By its own 1968 figures, GM admitted that 21,000 customers went unsatisfied in their complaints.) This indicates that down the line of corporate responsibility someone had those thoughts about cheapening the exhausts and disks, someone seconded those thoughts, and someone else carried them out. Death and injury resulted, and surely GM regrets it. Yet many millions in that $22 billion profit resulted also, and it is not likely that GM has regrets about that.

While it is impossible to know the wording of inter-office memos that carom back and forth between GM in-baskets, it is possible—using a plain ruler and common eyesight—to measure the effect of a cheapen-the-product decision. Consider the front bumper of the 1966 school bus, if a model in Washington, D.C., is representative. It is one-quarter-inch thick. On the 1969 model, it is one-eighth-inch thick. Thus in three years, the bumper's thickness was cut in half. Considering the thousands of buses manufactured with the thinner and cheaper bumper, the savings must have been considerable. But so was and is the risk of injury and death to the thousands of school children who might be better protected with the thicker bumper.

Incredibly, as if more blood could still be squeezed from this stone, the bumpers on these vehicles were the object of further GM cheapening. Behind the front bumpers of earlier models is a piece of steel extending from the frame in each direction about one foot, reinforcing the bumper. On the 1969 model, however, this piece of reinforcing steel is gone. Elsewhere on the same vehicle are other indications of the same cynical process. For example, any-one who wonders why the 1969 bus rides so roughly need only measure the leaf springs that support the body. Compared to those on earlier models, the springs are seven inches shorter.

If GM cheapens parts that a layman can detect, what may it have done to parts hidden under the hood and within the chassis? Here are management decisions that affect human lives far beyond the mere inconveniencing of customers, the mere cheating them of money. General Motors, as do its brother corporations like Ford, Chrysler, American Motors and the foreign motor companies, assures its customers that they can put their bodies into its product and go tearing off at high speeds. The average driver and his passengers, perhaps a little too blithely, never dream that any human being would sell them an unsafe car. Yet between 1966 and 1970, some 13,000,000 vehicles, or 36 percent of all vehicles manufactured, were recalled for possible defects. According to the Center for Auto Safety, GM led the list with 9,000,000 recalls. Auto executives are alert men, with pool-player minds wise to all angles; it is hardly possible they do not realize that a decision to cheapen may also be a decision to risk the lives of human beings. The exact number of accidents attributable to cheapening is unknowable, but with 56,000 killed by automobiles in 1970 and 4,500,000 wounded, it is reasonable to believe that not all the carnage was caused by drunk or wild driving. Much was doubtlessly caused by defective cars, and many of those defects resulted from decisions to cut costs.

One citizen who experienced the cheapness of a GM product was John Donovan. Unlike most owners, who have only themselves or their families to account for when they drive a GM vehicle, Donovan had responsibility for some 250 school children. These were the elementary and high-school students he transported to and from eight private schools in the vicinity of Washington, D.C. Ever since the famous Huntsville, Alabama, crash in May 1968, when the brakes of a GM school bus failed, killing one child, Donovan watched his vehicles carefully, servicing them frequently, driving carefully. At the time of the Huntsville tragedy, Donovan owned two GM buses, and he wanted no injuries or deaths due to faulty equipment, brakes or anything else.

A short, broad-chested man of thirty-six, born in Oklahoma, a former Marine Corps drill sergeant, brusque in speech, Donovan came to Washington as a student at Georgetown University. He stayed on, married and wound up teaching at a private school—Ascension Academy in Alexandria, Virginia. Students there describe Donovan as a friendly, approachable man with great skills at fairness and discipline; the graduating seniors twice voted him Ascension's most popular teacher.

Donovan began in the bus business in 1963 when a neighbor in the northwest section of Washington asked him if he would, for a fee, take his child to and from Ascension every day. Donovan agreed. After taking out the proper commercial-carrier insurance, he soon had other requests for the same service. The next two years, he used a station wagon and a Volkswagen microbus. By the 1968–69 school year, Donovan's business had grown; he spent $5000 dollars to purchase a 1966 General Motors 60-passenger bus and a 1959 Chevrolet 37-passenger model.

In the spring of 1969, the chance to expand still further came along, so that with more school buses he could transport 260 children to eight local private schools. The average yearly fare was $200. Many of the children in Donovan's buses were the sons and daughters of senators, ambassadors, judges, prominent lawyers, doctors and other important and powerful Washingtonians. Encouraged by his wife and with confidence in his capacity for hard work, Donovan decided to buy three new 1969 GMC-V-6 school buses. Each cost $8146.80. The body part of the buses was made by an independent company; everything else—basically the transmission, the wheels, the engine, the electrical system, the gas tank—came from General Motors Truck and Coach Division, Pontiac, Michigan.

Early in September 1969, Donovan went to High Point, North Carolina, to pick up his three new buses. Accompanying him were two drivers, as well as a GM dealer in Laurel, Maryland, from whom Donovan was buying the vehicles. On the return trip from High Point to Washington, Donovan had what he called at the time "a little trouble." One bus required sixteen quarts of oil for the 300-mile trip, somewhat beyond the normal thirst—one quart of oil per 1000 miles—of a vehicle this size. On the second bus, things went fine until the accelerator spring snapped. This meant that the driver had to put the transmission into neutral, find a place to pull over, get out, lift the hood and, with the engine racing and roaring, adjust the throttle spring with a pair of pliers. The third bus worked well until dusk, when the driver switched on the headlights. They didn't work.

All of this irritated Donovan, but he was forgiving. He knew enough about mechanics to understand that kinks are part of the new product and no cause for alarm. Except for rattling transmissions—which he couldn't understand, since heavy rattling was hardly dismissible as a kind of newness—Donovan's buses functioned normally for three days. He and his wife were proud of the buses. They had risked most of their savings on them and believed that no finer company existed than GM. Donovan named the three buses after his wife, Virginia, and their daughters, Regina and Colleen.

In mid-September, as required by law, Donovan took the vehicles to be inspected before using them to carry children. One bus passed, two did not. One rejection was caused by a faulty brake-hose suspension. General Motors, Donovan believed, either did not install the right part or did not install any part. Thus, the brake hose, which is essential for stopping and which should be suspended several inches away from the wheel, was rubbing the wheel drag line on turns. Amazed at how a well-known corporation like GM could let a slip like this occur, Donovan was nevertheless grateful that the inspectors had caught it.

"Thank God," he said to his wife. "Otherwise, the rubbing eventually would have broken the hose, and the brakes could have failed."

The second bus did not pass inspection because the exhaust-pipe hanger was faulty. This caused the lengthy exhaust pipe to dangle, increasing the chances of its snapping. If it had snapped, deadly carbon monoxide would have gushed out beneath the passenger compartment. "I thought the inspectors would be astonished, as I was," said Donovan, "that two brand-new General Motors buses, serviced by a GMC dealer, would fail to pass inspection. But they weren't surprised at all. They just said, 'Go get them fixed and come try again.'"

His amazement and annoyance slowly turned to dismay. For Donovan was serious about his responsibility for the lives of the children who rode his buses. Aside from the Huntsville tragedy, Donovan knew of other failures of GM buses. Only the year before, eighteen children from the Accotink Academy, of Springfield, Virginia, were riding in a new GM bus on highway 236 in the Washington suburb of Annandale. The brakes failed. Somehow, the driver managed to steer clear of traffic and coast the bus to a stop without an accident. The vehicle was subsequently fixed three times by a GM garage for brake trouble. The next year another Accotink bus, a 1969 GM, was being driven along a Fairfax County highway when the brakes failed completely. The driver lurched his way into a pasture to stop. *Those were new GM buses,* Donovan thought to himself, *and these three buses I just bought are new GMs too.* His mind easily pictured one of his buses, full of children, crashing into a tree, or into an oncoming car or truck. He became even more determined to do all he could to keep his three new buses in the best condition possible.

That commitment was made early in Donovan's ordeal, even though he had no way of knowing exactly what it would cost him—in loss of money, time and peace. Between September 6 and December 6, 1969, according to his diary, Donovan spent more than 225 hours either repairing the buses himself or hauling them to Central Motors, a GM dealership in Alexandria, for repairs. This averaged out to more than two hours daily, seven days a week. Additionally, he had to pay three of his drivers to do an extra ninety hours of repair work and hauling. A pattern emerged. When the buses finished the afternoon run about 4:30 or 5 P.M. and came to the lot in Washington where the drivers parked them overnight, Donovan would ask what, if anything, had broken or malfunctioned that day. The drivers would tell him, for example, that the clutch was burning out for the second time, or that the left rear tire had leaked air the way it had leaked air the day before, or that the bolts were falling out of the motor mounts the way they had last week, or that the wheels were wobbling, or that the power steering had failed.

The waking nightmare would now begin. Donovan would get in the broken bus and head for Central in Alexandria. Donovan's wife and two daughters would follow in the family car, so they could take him home when the bus was dropped off. It was a half-hour trip each way from Donovan's apartment in northwest Washington to Central Motors. After telling the mechanics what needed repairing, Donovan and family would come home. The children would be fed and put to bed. He and his wife, staring at each other numbly, would have supper. Then came the call from Central—which stayed open until 2 A.M. The Donovans would wake the children—no sitters were available at that hour—dress them, get in the car and head for Alexandria. Donovan would get the repaired bus and drive it to the lot in Washington, his wife and two children tailing. His records show that he did this approximately twenty-five times in the first three months of ownership. On occasion, two buses malfunctioned on the same day, so two round trips were needed. Sometimes, since he needed to be up at 5:45 every morning to call the drivers for the morning run, Donovan got only three hours' sleep. Both he and his wife lost weight during this period, as well as their sense of humor. Friends found the couple unusually snappish. Small wonder; among other deprivations, Donovan and his wife went out to dinner only twice in three months, and to the movies not at all.

As Donovan made repeated visits to Central Motors, a pattern soon emerged: The repairs he needed were seldom covered by the warranty. Trying to plug the dike through which money would trickle and eventually flood, Donovan traveled to Laurel, Maryland, to talk with the dealer from whom he bought the buses. "The dealer," said Donovan, "told me my buses were obviously special cases, that these problems certainly weren't universal. Nothing could be done, said the dealer, except notify the factory repre-

sentative. Donovan called the General Motors public relations office in Washington and was told the man who
would help him was John Nickell, the General Motors
truck-and-coach field representative for the Washington
area.

Between the breakdowns of his buses, Donovan tried
locating Nickell. He called several garages that were, according to the local office, on Nickell's list of places to
stop. Always the response was the same: Nickell had either
just left or was expected any minute. Donovan never found
his man this way. Finally, in a stake-out, he went one
morning to the dealer's garage in Laurel where, said the
owner, Nickell was scheduled to appear that afternoon.

He did. Donovan, momentarily elated at talking to a live
GM face, detailed the problems, from the burned out
clutches to the leaky gas tanks. According to Donovan,
Nickell's reaction at this meeting and the several to follow
was astonishment—no other operators in his area were
having these troubles; therefore, aside from warranty work,
GM could not be held responsible. "It must be my drivers,
Nickell told me," said Donovan. Up against this wall and
wanting his conscience to be clear should any of the buses
ever crash and kill anyone, Donovan wrote a letter to the
parents of the children he served. "In order to facilitate
safe transportation for your children with a minimum of
maintenance expense," said the letter, "I purchased three
new 1969 GMC buses in September of 1969. It verges on
the impossible to run the routes safely and on time. The
reason is that these three new GM buses continue to break
down. The vehicles have been fixed, re-fixed and re-re-
fixed. These malfunctions are not minor. They are major
mechanical failures which often involve the safety of your

children." Donovan listed the problems, then concluded: "If this pattern continues, we will have to discontinue the service."

One of these letters happened to come my way. As a reporter for the Washington *Post* with an interest in auto safety, I knew about the Huntsville crash and also that GM buses were recalled in 1968 and 1969. My first impulse was to leave the mess alone, thinking that the National Highway Safety Bureau surely had an eye on GM and their buses. About that time, however, I learned that the Federal Bureau had only one man assigned full time to school buses—one man in the entire Government to keep watch on tens of thousands of vehicles carrying hundreds of thousands of children. Donovan, if he truly had a story, would likely never get to tell it to the man at NHSB. How could the latter possibly give priority, as the bureaucrats say, to one operator with three buses?

I called Donovan and asked if I could examine his records and look at his buses. After several meetings in his apartment, it appeared that his complaints were valid. In any event, his anguish was real. With a drawn face and tired voice, he seemed like a defeated man. He and his wife had put their savings into the buses, and now it all appeared lost. One evening, after school, Donovan asked me to take a drive with him in one of his lemons. "I'm only going to get it up to twenty miles an hour," he said, "and then I'll put on the brakes." When he applied the brakes, the bus halted with an abruptness that lurched me forward. "We were only going twenty," said Donovan, opening the door and going around back. On the road were two black skid marks. The two rear wheels had locked when Donovan put on the brakes. "Can you imagine what happens," he asked, "when a bus is going fifty or sixty and the driver has to stop suddenly?"

After again looking through Donovan's material, I approached General Motors to get their side of the story and give them a chance to be heard. I tried contacting John Nickell. I left my name at his office several times, but my calls were never returned. I visited Central Motors in Alexandria one morning—"He'll be there all day," said a secretary in his office—but like Donovan before me, I did not find Nickell that day or any other day. Garage workers at Central said that Richard Lockwood, the service manager, coordinated with Nickell and that perhaps he could help me.

I approached Lockwood. He preferred not talking about Donovan's problems. "General Motors has official spokesmen for questions from the public. You ought to ask them." When pressed for an explanation of why so many parts of Donovan's buses kept breaking or malfunctioning, Lockwood said, "Some of Donovan's problems are real, some are fanciful." Asked for an example of Donovan's fancy, Lockwood recalled a visit by Donovan when the latter said the clutch on one bus needed fixing. "We drove it around for a road test," said Lockwood, "and there was nothing wrong with it." When informed of Lockwood's statement, Donovan agreed; the mechanic did drive it around. "So I took the bus home, with no repairs made. Maybe Lockwood was right that time. But two days later, the clutch burned out."

At 6:45 on the evening of December 9, Donovan phoned me at home. "Guess what," he said with elation, the first happy note I had heard from him since our initial meeting. "GM finally knows I exist. Three of their men are coming over to see me in an hour. They said they want to talk things over with me about the buses. That's all they said." Donovan asked me if I could come over and sit in on the meeting; it might be interesting. I said yes, I'd be there in twenty minutes.

When I arrived, the Donovans were on the last bites of a meal of meat loaf, canned peas, apple sauce, bread and milk. Their apartment, a third-floor walkup in a northwest Washington housing project, was in mild disorder, a crib in the middle of the room, a chair holding a drawer filled with Donovan's records, a filing cabinet in a corner, and a card table covered with invoices, receipts and other papers. I asked Donovan why he thought GM wanted this meeting. "Hard to tell," he replied. "Maybe they see that my complaints are real and they finally want to square it all up. I've heard of things like that happening."

"I haven't," cut in Donovan's wife, Virginia, "especially not from a bunch like this. The bigger they get, the less they care." A short, sandy-haired woman, second-generation Polish, a user of short, bright sentences every syllable of which she intensely believes in, Virginia Donovan was perhaps the wearier of the two. Stashed in the apartment all day with the two children, she was the one who had to phone the parents when a bus broke down, to announce that their children would either not be picked up in the morning or be late in the afternoon. She had typed the December 8 letter as well as the earlier letters to GM president Edward N. Cole, Richard Nixon, Virginia Knauer, the Federal Trade Commission and the National Highway Safety Bureau. She also had opened and filed the depressing form-letter replies. "It'll be a snow job, John," she

said. "Just wait and see. The drifts will be so high not even
a bus could drive through."

Donovan speculated that GM had heard, probably from
Richard Lockwood or someone else at Central Motors, that
I was looking into the problem. "They hate bad publicity," he said. "Just the thought of a possible story in a
major newspaper has flushed them out. It's funny. GM
hasn't really been so bad. They've done a faithful job on
the work they say is covered by the warranty. The mechanics at Central are superb. I get fast service, they're
courteous. The eerie thing is that I can't find anyone who'll
take responsibility for what's gone wrong."

At 7:30, the GM men arrived. Donovan, putting the
infant in the crib and the three-year-old on a chair, went
to the door and opened it. "Hello, Mr. Donovan," said
the out-front man. "I'm Webb Madery of General Motors."
Round-faced, heavy in the waist, he rubbed his hands
briskly and commented on the cold outside. Madery introduced Jerry Fender and John Nickell. Donovan invited
them in. The three were cheery, almost bouncy. Donovan
introduced them to Virginia. Madery, with a large smile,
said that he was happy to finally meet Mrs. Donovan and
that everything her husband had said about her certainly
seemed true. The woman did not respond to Madery's
pleasantry. She knew her husband had spoken with him
on the phone several times, but she also knew her husband
had never mentioned her to an official of a corporation
the young couple had come to loathe. "What a nice little
place you have here," said Madery, not letting up. He was
unaware that the housewife didn't consider her apartment
"nice" at all; she had told me five minutes before that her
family would have moved into a house that fall if repairing

the three buses had not consumed so much of her and her husband's money, time and emotions. Still icily mum, she took the gentlemen's coats and hung them up.

Of the trio, Madery was the oldest—sixty-two—and, as the Washington zone manager, was highest on GM's ladder. His career in the automobile industry began in 1933. After one year of college at William and Mary, he worked for International Harvester, then Chrysler. In 1958, he accepted an offer from General Motors to become heavy duty truck manager in the Detroit zone. A year later he moved to Washington.

Fender, a trim, short-haired man of fifty-eight, had the longest GM service of the three, having begun in Oakland as a twenty-four-year-old factory helper. Slowly rising from the bottom, he advanced to shop clerk, parts manager, and so on, eventually coming to Washington as zone service and parts manager.

Nickell, forty-nine and with prematurely gray hair, had started with GM in 1940 on the assembly line in the Pontiac truck plant. During this time, he went to school, earning a B.A. in history from the Detroit Institute of Technology. Then he became a parts supervisor and began his climb.

Standing in the uncarpeted living room of the Donovan apartment and not yet down to business, the three GM men continued their cheeriness. They said they had just come from a delightful meal whose main dish was pheasant-under-glass. "You'd really like pheasant," said Madery to Mrs. Donovan with an overwarm smile, apparently determined to thaw her somehow.

Moving from the living room into the adjoining part of the L-shaped area, Donovan introduced the three officials to me. I stated clearly that I was a Washington *Post* reporter and had begun investigating Donovan's troubles. Still engaged in the busy-work of cordiality, the GM men did not seem to notice the significance of having a reporter on hand while they went about the work of customer relations. Of the three, however, John Nickell, an alert, lively-eyed man, did look twice at me. My name may have been familiar, perhaps from the message slips of my phone calls. Yet after shaking hands with me at the Donovan apartment, Nickell, lowest of the three in actual corporate power but closest to the daily problems of Donovan, seemed to let the fact of my presence pass. If his superiors weren't concerned, why should he be?

Everyone gathered around a small dining-room table, everyone except Mrs. Donovan. She sat on a living-room chair within hearing distance and took out yellow scratch paper, ready to take in shorthand the important remarks of the conversation. The General Motors men produced a folder of records covering what they said was the past twelve weeks of Donovan's ownership of the three buses. As the senior official, Madery led off, explaining cordially that the purpose of the meeting was that "GM wanted to make things right." He said that his corporation had a long record of being concerned about producing safe vehicles, especially those that carry children, and that since Donovan was concerned about safety, GM was most concerned about him. GM, he said, likes to satisfy its customers.

Impatiently, Donovan broke in. "I've heard all that talk before," he said. "What I'd like from GM right now is a detailed record of the repairs you've made on my buses and also the modifications you've made on them." Donovan's request, made in a low but firm voice, was based on a desire to keep an accurate maintenance record. He explained to his audience that "this is the same as wanting information from your surgeon about what he cuts or takes out while operating on your insides. How can you find out unless the surgeon tells you?" Madery, the wings of his good humor making a final flap of fun, laughed at this, saying with a happy grin that he had had operations where the surgeon never told him what he had fooled with. Donovan didn't laugh. On seeing this, Madery nodded to Nickell. "Mr. Donovan should certainly have his records," said Madery. "That's only fair." Nickell said he would get them to Donovan later that week without fail.

As the GM-Donovan case unfolded over the next year, the company never supplied Donovan the records he repeatedly asked for and which GM repeatedly promised. In the week immediately after the December 9 meeting in the apartment, Donovan says, he was told by Jerry Fender that high-level officials in Detroit had made a decision not to release the records "at this time in these circumstances." The circumstances were that my series of articles on Donovan and his plight had just begun in the Washington *Post* and had been relayed by its wire service. Donovan believed GM refused to release the enormous record of work, repairs and replacements on the grounds that the public—specifically other owners—would learn of it and thus expect similar treatment. As for who in GM ordered the embargo, Donovan never learned. At a meeting in January 1970, in Falls Church, Virginia, with Robert Stelter, general sales manager for the GM Truck and Coach Division in Pontiac, Michigan, who entered the case when it became a public issue, the question again came up. Donovan says he asked Stelter directly why GM had refused to release the records. Stelter, the superior of Madery, said he himself never understood why not. He directed John Nickell, also present at this meeting, to pass along the records. Nickell said he would, but he never did.

At the December 9 apartment gathering, the next topic was an itemized reading by Nickell of the repairs made at GM's expense. The list was long—including leaking oil gaskets, broken motor mounts, flawed gasoline tanks, ruptured rear-wheel seals, uneven brakes, bad tires, wobbly wheels, weak tailpipe hangers—and anyone not knowing the whole story would wonder why Donovan was complaining when GM had done all this work free of charge.

"What about those tailpipe hangers?" asked Donovan. Nickell, shooting a confident glance at his boss as if to say the question was a routine grounder and easily fielded, replied that GM had replaced them on warranty. "I know that," said Donovan, "but the replacements were the same design as the original ones. So where does that take me?" For my benefit and looking at me, Nickell explained in layman's terms the nature of a tailpipe hanger: a metal straplike device hung from the frame of the bus and attached to the exhaust pipe to keep it from dragging along the road and breaking.

At this point, the smooth GM presentation showed signs, like Donovan's buses, of falling apart. The customer insisted on getting across his point that replacing a flawed hanger with another flawed hanger, however new, is not really a victory for safety. Visibly annoyed at wrangling over such a small item and apparently sensing a no-win situation, Nickell broke in to admit that "the hangers were just not strong enough. The factory made them too flimsy."

Madery looked sharply at Nickell—either startled or

angered at this frank concession. He jumped in to say that studies of the hanger were already under way in Detroit and that a better one was being designed. Donovan said he was happy to hear that. He asked, however, if GM was going to warn other owners of 1969 GM buses around the country that this particular part was made "too flimsy." Madery said the decision would have to be made by higher-ups in Detroit. "I'm sure they'll tell the public," said Donovan, "because, as you say, GM cares about its customers and the safety of children." That was sarcasm, but not without a basis in fact. As of eighteen months after this conversation, the flimsy tailpipe hangers still had not been recalled.

All GM cheerfulness was now defunct. The next topic involved the leaky gasoline tanks on Donovan's buses. Nickell reminded Donovan that three weeks earlier, to show GM's good faith, he had promised to repair the leaky tanks free of charge. That was a gesture of pure largesse, Nickell made clear, because GM did not make the tank. Madery looked pleased. Nickell's statement backed up Madery's earlier one of "making things right."

"I'm not impressed," said Donovan, his anger growing. "After you told me that GM didn't make the gas tank that was leaking, I called up Thomas Body [Thomas Body Company, High Point, North Carolina, the firm which produced the bus shells on Donovan's buses and had fitted them onto the GM chassis]. Mr. Thomas personally told me —categorically—that his company does not make the tank, GM does."

Nickell could do nothing but admit error. Coming back fast, however, Madery explained to Donovan that even though Nickell was wrong about the maker of the tank, it actually didn't matter, because the leak was later found by mechanics not to be in the GM-made tank but in the extension from the tank to the exterior of the bus. "That is a Thomas product," said Madery firmly. He said that GM had nothing to do with it.

Donovan could not argue, at least not then. The next morning, however, he was on the phone again to John Thomas. I also called Thomas within the week. Thomas said, with no equivocation, that his company did not make the tank-neck extension, that it was a GM product. To be certain, I asked him to check his file and read over the phone Donovan's order page; it was number 9-12202, and the facts again fit. A few days after the apartment meeting, Donovan reported to the GM men what he learned from Thomas. The officials, according to Donovan, "just kind of passed it off, admitting they were in 'error' again but attaching no importance to it. But I attached plenty of importance to it. I was being lied to. Not by men who had any reason to gain from the lies, but because it was corporate policy. Put me down, brush me off, keep me happy—but don't ever tell me the truth or give me new buses."

As the meeting continued—Donovan running through his list of complaints, GM running through their list of solutions—the question came up of whether or not these problems were limited to Donovan's buses. They had to be, said Madery; otherwise, GM would have heard from other owners. "What about Tom Gist and Billy Jubb?" asked Donovan, referring to two owners of 1969 GM school buses, in nearby Maryland, with whom he had spoken at length recently about their mechanical and safety problems. Donovan said both men were experiencing difficulties similar to his own and that both said they had seen John Nickell. His memory refreshed, Nickell said that was right, he had seen Gist and Jubb. Their problems, however, were different from Donovan's, said Nickell. Once again, Donovan could not argue back with absolute surety. The following day, I called Thomas Gist in Sykesville, Maryland, the owner of two '69 GMs. As with Donovan's buses, the power steering was bad, riding was rough, the clutches and brakes needed constant adjustment and fixing. I mentioned Donovan's name. Gist recognized it, laughingly saying they were fellow sufferers. Billy Jubb, Pasadena, Maryland, owned four '69s and called them "the worst I've ever owned." Each had a broken clutch. What he said about clutches echoed John Donovan: "I'm always taking the damn things to the dealer to have them adjusted."

"How does GM explain all these failures of clutches?" Donovan asked Madery. "Driver abuse," replied the GM man, starting out on a brief monologue on the many ways drivers ride the clutch, pump it unnecessarily, use it wrongly. Donovan replied, again with anger, that his drivers were not heavy-footed amateurs who loved clutch-riding, but were veterans of the road with at least five years' experience in driving trucks and buses. None had ever burned out a clutch on earlier-year buses. Thus, said Donovan, it was unlikely they would have ruined the clutches at the rate they were being ruined on the new buses: Two had already burned out in two buses; three had burned out in the third.

The talk went back and forth, Donovan repeating his concern for safe buses because children's lives were involved, Madery cordially reassuring him that GM had made

things right with its warranty work and that this was a
fluke problem. He had a way of feigning surprise, as if to
say wordlessly to Donovan, "You're not actually saying,
are you, that GM is not 'the mark of excellence'?" Not
once did Madery or his two companions offer sympathy
to Donovan, or ever admit there might be a safety problem. If a problem was admitted, it was inevitably "not
safety-related." On specific problems, the reply was either,
"Here, this is what GM has done, so why are you complaining?" or, "Here, you should have done this, and if you
had, this problem would never have happened." Nor did
the GM men ever acknowledge that their buses had been
the object of recalls two years running, and that this year
was an extension of patterns of work developed then.

As the hour neared 10 P.M., Donovan was still spirited,
but Madery, Fender and Nickell, the taste of pheasant
long gone, were tiring. As they tried to wind things down,
the phone rang. Mrs. Donovan, another willing all-nighter,
answered. "It's for you, John, from Detroit, person-to-
person." Donovan took the phone and was greeted by
Robert Stelter, general sales manager of the GM Truck
and Coach Division, and Madery's superior. "He wants to
know how things are going with my buses," Donovan remarked to the group. Answering Stelter, he said the buses
were just as much broken-down lemons as ever. The two
talked for about five minutes, Donovan asking for his records and repeating that he worried about his brakes,
clutches, gas tanks, wheels and everything else that
wouldn't stay fixed, no matter GM's diligence in repairing
them.

I signaled Donovan that I would like a word with
Stelter. Identifying myself and my intentions clearly, I

asked Stelter how three new buses could become so flawed so quickly. The company, he replied, was doing all it could to make things right. Beyond making things right, I asked politely, would GM make things better and do as Donovan thought it should do—replace the buses? The official seemed surprised Donovan had even had the thought.

After showing curiosity over what kind of story I might be writing but careful to remain pleasant and assuring, Stelter asked to speak to Madery. As GM Detroit spoke to GM Washington, there was little but yes-sirs and no-sirs from the latter. Madery concluded his conversation by saying he would call Stelter in the morning. The phone hardly back on the receiver, the GM official looked at me in astonishment: "You're a reporter?" I nodded. Nickell nodded too.

Abruptly, the GM men began putting away the materials they had spread out on the table during the evening. The phone call from Detroit, apparently meant as final proof to Donovan that GM really cared—because his troubles had reached the ears of high powers in Detroit—had had the opposite effect. GM had learned that rather than having put down a customer, it had instead fired up a customer, one who had the crust to interest a reporter in his troubles.

Madery rose, as did Nickell and Fender, and recapturing his earlier verve, smiled broadly at Donovan and said that the evening was certainly well spent. Madery even had one last happy word for Mrs. Donovan, throwing her a compliment about "what wonderful boys" the Donovan's two baby girls were. Donovan got the men their coats and saw them to the door.

I remained for a few minutes. Mrs. Donovan said, "Let's

get the snow shovels and clear out this place." Her husband saw the evening a little less bitterly. GM now knew, he said, that it could not talk its way out of it. "They didn't refute a fact I threw at them. That's the test. They would have slapped me down hard if one fact of mine, one record or one document, was slightly off. But they didn't. Sure, they tried to scare me off, calm me down. What do you expect?"

After telling Donovan I would call him in a few days to check if anything had happened, I said good night.

On December 15 and 22, 1969, I wrote two stories in the *Post* on Donovan's ordeal. On the day of the second story, General Motors and the White House Office of Consumer Affairs held a joint press conference to announce two investigations of the 1969 buses, one by the Government and the other by the company. The press conference statements of GM vice-president Martin Caserio were oddly similar to the GM presentation at the Donovan apartment. Caserio said there were no complaints about the buses from other owners. Asked about the '69 buses that suffered brake failure and careened into a pasture, Caserio said he believed the braking equipment on that vehicle was not the same as that on Donovan's, although "I'm not certain about that yet." Like Madery, Caserio stressed GM's concern for safety. Thus, the faulty exhaust-pipe hangers should not be classified as safety-related defects, because if they broke the driver could hear the exhaust pipe clattering along the ground and have repairs made before any harm was done to occupants. (But what if they merely cracked?)

Reporters pressed Caserio on Donovan's problems. For the first time, the company gave a little, Caserio conceding that some of Donovan's complaints were legitimate. But always added to these admissions was the qualifier, "They are not safety-related." One reporter listed all of Donovan's problems—from brakes to clutches—and said Caserio's claiming these were nonsafety problems was an "incredible observation." The press conference did produce one memorable statement: "GM," said Caserio, does "not duck any responsibility for the finished product that bears our name."

Two months later, on February 19, 1970, 4269 finished school buses were officially recalled by General Motors, including the three of John Donovan and including 21,681 trucks using the same model chassis. "Some of the vehicles," said the announcement, "will require installation of new brake-hose retaining springs. Some will require inspection and possible inspection and possible alignment or replacement of a rear steel brake line. A few will require both services."

At my request, GM sent me a list of forty-four owners around the country who operated more than five buses. In calling them—except for four people who in reality were not GM owners and one owner who couldn't be reached because he had been dead four years—a recurring theme was clutch problems. One owner was a GM dealer who had so much trouble with his seven 1969s that in 1970 he bought Fords. Asked if he thought it odd that a GM dealer should buy a competitor's product, he answered, "What should I do—keep on buying buses that I know are nothing but trouble?"

Within the next year, the GM buses were recalled two more times. The second call-in involved the brakes again —possibly faulty brake-fluid reservoirs which caused the braking fluid to leak out. The third recall was for possibly flawed clutches; the clutch linkage was found to be weak —meaning, in lay terms, that the bus could lock in gear and thus not be stoppable.

Friends of Donovan, who found him somewhat more cheerful after the third recall, jokingly called him a "giant-killer," since he had taken on GM and won. "Won? How can they say that?" he asks. "I never got new replacements from GM for my buses. I never got a cent for my lost time. They never compensated my drivers for the overtime spent in hauling the buses to the garage. They never even apologized to my wife for all those nights she spent trailing me over to Central Motors. What's even more chilling, after three recalls, I have yet to hear from the GM crowd even the slightest hint admitting they may be doing something wrong in the way they build buses. But lives are involved; those are not alarm clocks they're selling. That's the true horror of all this—not that they tried to screw one owner like me. It's the corporate callousness. If I were in the business of making school buses—an engineer, a vice-president, a local representative like Madery—and someone came along with proof that dangerous defects were in my product, well, I think I'd jump pretty quick to correct them before I had any blood on my hands."

In a simpler day a consumer with a complaint about, say, shoes, had only to visit the local shoemaker to get justice. "Here," he would say, "these shoes are falling apart." The shoemaker, being either ethical or aware that word would spread through the village about his sloppy work, quickly replaced or repaired the shoes. The exchange was straightforward, with no evasions. What's more, the shoemaker was *there;* he had a familiar face; he breathed, and the only separation between the consumer and him was his shop counter.

Things have changed. The agony of seeking relief or redress from GM, with its 750,000 employees, is the same as seeking it from any large bureaucracy. The vice-presidents at the top are protected from the consumer's complaints at the bottom by a mass of employees in between; the latter will catch it first if the brass learns that the consumers are mad. So the vice-presidents are free to measure the company's success not by the consumer's voice—the way the shoemaker did—but by sales reports, profit charts and the smiles of stockholders. If tens of thousands of cars are sold every year, the high-ups conclude that the public must be happy; otherwise, why are sales up? When profits aren't up, however, or when management thinks they can be better, a decision is inevitably made in favor of cheapening the product. When the result of such a decision may be death, then the ethical numbness encouraged by the profit system becomes grimly apparent.

In a recent conversation with a GM official about another matter, I asked in passing whether he had heard lately from John Donovan. "Oh no," said the GM man, "that's all in the past. We served Donovan well." I passed along the comment to Donovan. He smiled. "I lived on a farm when I was a kid," he said, "so I know what GM means when they say they served me."

CHAPTER THREE

A Colonial Heritage

by **MORTON MINTZ**

ABOUT a decade ago, nine major oil companies undertook to build a long, costly pipeline for gasoline, home-heating fuels, and other petroleum products. To accomplish this task the companies—Cities Service, Continental, Gulf, Mobil, Phillips, Standard of Indiana, Sinclair, Texaco, and Union—set up a corporate instrument called the Colonial Pipeline Company. Headquartered in Atlanta, Colonial Pipeline was formally chartered in 1962. By 1966, according to *Fortune* magazine's annual listing of the 500 largest industrial corporations, the combined assets of the owning companies were $31,768,415,000. Texaco, the largest of Colonial's proprietors, ranked fourth among all industrial corporations; Cities Service, the smallest, ranked thirtieth. By 1968, the combined assets of the nine companies exceeded $35 billion, an increase of more than $3 billion in only two years.

A venture that such giants felt it necessary to undertake jointly might reasonably be expected to be of substantial size. This one is substantial indeed. It is twice as large as any petroleum-products pipeline built previously. The main line is 1531 miles long, but there are also 1315 miles of stub lines to serve terminals in thirteen states. For those who derive a mental image of "pipe" from household plumbing, it should be noted that the word has but a slight relationship to this conduit. Between the starting point of the main line in Houston, Texas, and the terminus in Linden, New Jersey, the pipeline measures as much as one yard in diameter. The capacity of the line is up to 1,000,000 barrels per day—enough, say, to fill the tanks of roughly 2,500,000 automobiles. The cost of the pipeline, approximately $390 million, made it the largest privately financed construction project in history. Simon H. Rifkind, counsel for Colonial, once said that the $390 million "is more than the United States paid out for the construction of the Panama Canal."

To run their $390-million enterprise, the oil companies that owned Colonial, through their representatives on the board of directors, chose Ben David Leuty, then fifty-nine, who had been president of Cities Service Pipeline Company. After a brief period as Colonial's vice-president for construction, he was named president. Was Leuty not chosen, attorney Rifkind would ask later, "because his reputation was as stainless as the very reputation of this Colonial Pipeline is stainless . . . because they knew his character to be beyond reproach and his reputation to be free of stain?"[1] On another occasion, Rifkind said that in Leuty "I found a man whom I learned greatly to admire and deeply to love . . . a man of impeccable character both in speech and in conduct."

To be executive vice-president, the directors of Colonial selected Karl T. Feldman, then fifty-two, who had been an official of Sinclair Pipeline Company. An engineer, he had spent thirty-five years in the oil industry. Adrian M. Foley, Jr., a lawyer who came to know Feldman well, has described him as a "family man . . . [a] church man, a quiet man . . ." He has, Foley said, "a record of spotless accomplishment attributable to one thing only, steadfastness, integrity and hard work."

In addition to Feldman, Sinclair Pipeline gave up its general manager of operations, Glenn H. Giles, to Colonial, initially as manager of construction, reporting to Ben Leuty, and then as vice-president of operations. Mobil Pipeline Company loaned Fred Stewart, who had been with it since 1939 and who before that was prosecuting attorney of Douglas County, Missouri, to supervise acquisition of rights of way from the Potomac River in Maryland to the terminus of the pipeline in New Jersey.

The point need not be belabored: The major oil companies transfused some of their best men into the Colonial Pipeline Company.

Colonial needed a "tank farm," a place where petroleum products piped in from Texas would be received, stored as long as necessary in twenty-two huge tanks, and then

---

[1] This quotation, and others that follow which are not specifically attributed, was taken from public records the nature of which will be made clear shortly.

distributed to individual oil companies. Starting around September 1962, Colonial was searching for a site. Within a few months it was seriously considering four possibilities. All were in or around Woodbridge, New Jersey, which, with a population of about 100,000, was the seventh-largest community in the state. In February 1963, Colonial reached an agreement *in principle* to buy for $1.4 million a 177-acre site on the west side of the New Jersey Turnpike owned by the Shell Oil Company. But not until several months thereafter, on July 18, 1963—a critical date, as will be seen—did Colonial make a $70,000 down payment and legally obligate itself to buy the property. In the meantime, the company undertook to make sure of two things: that Shell's title to the land was absolutely clear, and that the tanks could be built if the property were acquired.

In early June 1963, about six weeks before Colonial contracted to buy the Shell property, Fred Stewart, the rights-of-way buyer, went to the Municipal Building in Woodbridge. There, he paid a call on Mayor Walter Zirpolo. Zirpolo was a real estate entrepreneur and investor who had made a fortune building a chain of supermarkets and whose home—in an area called Colonia—was well-known for its indoor swimming pool and a waterfall that cascaded down an interior wall.

Stewart has said that he introduced himself, told Zirpolo that Colonial was negotiating with Shell Oil for the 177-acre property, and asked how he should proceed to get a building permit to erect twenty-two tanks on the site.

"The Mayor said we had come in an awfully bad time," Stewart recalled. The residents of the north side of Woodbridge "don't want any more tankage up there," Zirpolo told Stewart, adding, "I have promised the people that there will be no more." The Mayor pointed out that there would have to be a public hearing before a permit could be granted and warned Stewart: "Just bear in mind that nothing is to be done about this until after the election in November."

"I thanked him for his kindness," Stewart said. After he left, he phoned Atlanta to tell his boss, L. P. Humann, manager of Colonial's right-of-way department, "what we were up against."

The obstacles to getting a permit were even greater than the Mayor had indicated. In 1961, as leader of a group of young Democrats that displaced an old guard, Zirpolo had charged that his rivals had "betrayed" north side residents "and sold them out to the petroleum interests." Now Zirpolo and his friend Robert E. Jacks, president of the Township Committee (later, the Town Council), were seeking re-election. "Tanks? No Tanks!" said one of the flyers they distributed in the months preceding the election. "There will be no tanks in your residential area now or at any time that the Zirpolo administration serves you on the Town Committee. That is the solemn pledge of men you know you can trust."

On July 22, 1963, four days after Colonial Pipeline closed the deal for the Shell Oil tract, Stewart and Humann paid a second visit to the Mayor. They showed him "an artist's conception" of the "tank farm." According to Stewart, the discussion included "the possibility of putting plantings on the turnpike side so it wouldn't be visible to the public so much, to kind of hide it, to make it pretty." Zirpolo reminded his visitors of "the trouble we are having with the people" on the north side, the residents of the Third Ward in the Port Reading section. Stewart and Humann were about to leave when the Mayor, while looking at the artist's rendering, was struck by an idea that might help "to quiet the people down," Stewart said. There was to be a control building in the "tank farm," and it would be visible to the public from the turnpike. The building was to be a standardized metal prefab. But if, instead, it were to be " 'colonial' architecture," Zirpolo said, "it would be in keeping with the company name, and it would be a thing of beauty. It wouldn't be such an eyesore."

The Colonial Pipeline executives left a few minutes later, after Zirpolo said that they should not yet apply for a building permit, and that the required public hearing on such an application continued to be "your big problem." Once out of the city hall, Humann phoned Atlanta to ask Colonial's chief engineer "to start digging up some plans for 'colonial' designs." Stewart thought a resurrection of the eighteenth century along the turnpike would "look out of place and kind of silly." But he went along, nettled by the knowledge that thousands of dollars in needless expense would have to be incurred.

Stewart made a third visit to the city hall a few weeks later, on August 16. This time he was alone. He showed Zirpolo a revised plan. The control building was still a metal prefab, but it had been moved from the edge to the center of the "tank farm" so that it could not be seen from the turnpike. "All right," the Mayor said, "we'll forget the 'colonial' architecture." The conversation then turned to the great obstacle in the path of the pipeline company, the public hearing on a building permit. Stewart recalled the dialogue this way:

I said, "If there is any way in the world to avoid a public hearing, if there is another ordinance we could get under, just anything to avoid a public hearing, we need to do that."

He says, "I'll tell you what. I think it's time that you ought to see Mr. Jacks."

He said, "Do you know Mr. Jacks?"

I said, "No, I don't know Mr. Jacks."

He said, "He is the president of the Council. I'd like for you to go up there today and see him because he is expecting you."

He took out a card and wrote down Mr. Jacks's name and address.

He said, "Now, I'd go on up there if I were you. He is expecting you."

In a feature piece on Township Council president Robert Jacks, a reporter for the Perth Amboy *Evening News* said: "In his style of politics, Jacks has incorporated the best of the new and old schools of political theory and policies." The reporter, Henry J. Price, went on to say: "Natty in dress, charming in personality, Jacks presents the picture of a big-time political figure in a town that is moving into the big leagues in county and state politics."

Jacks, who was forty when the story was published in May 1965, had enlisted in the Marine Corps when he was eighteen. He had spent thirty-three months in the Pacific Theater and fought at Guadalcanal and in five other major campaigns, each time on D-Day. At Iwo Jima, three leaders of his platoon were killed successively in action, and on each occasion he had taken over. He had won a Bronze Star. After the war, Jacks and Mayor

Zirpolo had become very close. They had engaged in real-estate ventures together, and they had moved successfully into politics together in 1957. Jacks had owned Metro Motors, a used-car dealership in Woodbridge, since 1952. "I was in business a long time before I became a public official, and no one can point a finger at me for conflict of interest of any kind," Jacks told Henry Price.

Fred Stewart, of Colonial, drove over to Metro Motors, where he found Jacks and introduced himself. "Yes, I know all about it," Jacks said. As had the Mayor, Jacks emphasized the difficulties that a public hearing would pose. According to Stewart:

> He said, "You have got to have friends that will be able to pass this permit for you over the objections of the people."
>
> He said, "That's where you have got to get right."
>
> I said, "What do you mean by that?"
>
> "Well," he said, "we've got to have a campaign contribution."
>
> "Well," I said, "we don't make campaign contributions."
>
> "Well," he said, "you are going to have to in this instance if you get anywhere with your permit."
>
> "Well," I said, "we can't do it. It is unlawful. It is illegal, and we just don't do it and we can't do it."
>
> "Well," I said, "by way of curiosity, just how much are you talking about for the campaign contribution?"
>
> He said, "Fifty thousand."
>
> With that, I rolled up my map and I left. . . .
>
> The next thing I did, I got over on the turnpike and drove down to the first public telephone, first Howard Johnson Restaurant, and called Atlanta.

Stewart tried to reach Humann, but he was out. And so
Stewart spoke instead to Jack Vickrey, a vice-president of
Colonial and its general counsel. He told Vickrey what
had happened and described Jacks's demand as "unlawful."
Vickrey, Stewart said, agreed: ". . . that is unlawful, that
is illegal, and you know you can't do it." Vickrey, making
clear that to accede to the demand would be illegal "under
both Federal and State law," advised Stewart, "Stay away,
never go back, back off from it."

Four days later, Fred Stewart, phoning from Colonial's
office in Cherry Hill, New Jersey, finally reached Humann
in Atlanta. "Mr. Vickrey gave you awfully good advice,"
the Colonial executive said. "Don't go back. Stay away."
In turn, Humann passed the information along to Glenn
Giles, the construction manager, who went up one flight
of stairs to the office of Ben Leuty, the president. There,
Giles reported the situation to Leuty and Karl Feldman,
the executive vice-president.

The reactions of these two executives, and of Giles as
well, are important in determining whether they were
guilty of the serious crime of bribery or were merely the
victims of extortion. Giles later described the reactions of
the three men, first in a secret proceeding and then in a
public one. In the secret proceeding, he characterized the
situation as one in which "[we] were told that if we paid
the money they'd pass this thing over the residents' objections, jam it through." This was the tone of *realpolitik*.
Giles made no mention of any howl of outrage, which is
considered the normal reaction from victims of extortion,
and he did not in that secret proceeding, where he was
free to say what he willed, use such terms as "shakedown"
or "extortion." But in a subsequent proceeding, a public

one, Giles claimed he had told Leuty and Feldman, "The dirty bastards are shaking us down for fifty thousand dollars." He said that Leuty, "a mild-mannered man" who doesn't use the type of language I guess that I do sometimes," had been "agitated." And Feldman, he remembered, had "raised up and pounded the table and said, 'They can't do this to us.'"

The top officers of Colonial Pipeline delayed making a decision on Robert Jacks's demand for $50,000 for more than a week after it was reported to them on August 20, 1963. They held meetings at which, Glenn Giles later recalled, Ben Leuty, Karl Feldman, and himself "discussed the fact that we preferred not to get any more Colonial Pipeline Company people involved in this than we absolutely needed." In addition, Giles said, there was an unresolved problem of how to "acquire funds . . . that could be converted to cash." Finally, Giles said, Feldman "passed on" instructions to pay the $50,000.

The money was to be paid through a conduit, the Rowland Tompkins Corporation, of Hawthorne, New York, the firm that on July 11—a week before the Shell Oil site was purchased—was notified by Colonial that its bid of $637,000 was the successful one to build the "tank farm" and its pumping station. The president of the firm was Howard Tompkins, son of the founder. The only other officer was the vice-president, Ralph A. Bankes, husband of Tompkins' sister. The directors of the company were the two officers and their wives.

Bankes. Leuty. Jacks. The names are flamboyantly Dickensian. They also are the true names. Lest the reader suspect a put-on, let him be cautioned now that he has yet to meet William L. Fallow and, yes, Harry F. Waste.

On about September 1, following his instructions from
the executive vice-president of Colonial, Giles phoned Roy
A. Murphy, a representative of Rowland Tompkins whom
he had known for a year or two. Giles asked Murphy's
help in acquiring the $50,000 and making the payments,
telling Murphy that the money was to be given to a public
official of Woodbridge in order to get a building permit.
Giles added that "the city officials would not accept our
building permit application until after Election Day"—
November 5. "He heard me out, and then told me that
he would have to talk with his people," Giles said afterward.

A few days later, in a phone call to Atlanta, Murphy
said that his firm would cooperate, but only because
it wanted the $637,000 contract. "He informed me,"
Giles said, "that they very reluctantly agreed that they
would handle this inasmuch as they were quite anxious to
get the job started." Over the next few years, Colonial
awarded Rowland Tompkins additional contracts for about
$1.3 million.

Giles and Murphy, after a preliminary meeting in
Atlantic City, met in Atlanta, at Colonial's offices in
the Lenox Towers at 3390 Peachtree Road North East.
There, on blank Rowland Tompkins stationery Murphy
had brought along, they composed a letter and addressed
it to Karl Feldman. Murphy signed it. Feldman and Ben
Leuty initialed it. The letter served as an agreement to
expand the original contract to include work by Rowland
Tompkins that it would never do: phony work. Colonial
agreed to pay the contractor $108,000. Of this, Rowland

Tompkins would need $58,000 for Federal and state taxes. Thus it would be left with the tax-free $50,000 it needed to pay Robert Jacks.

Giles said that he and Murphy agreed to have Colonial pay the $50,000 not in a lump sum, but in three installments: one, of $20,000, shortly after Election Day; one, of $15,000, when Colonial received a building permit; and one, also of $15,000, when Colonial received a certificate of occupancy. Each time Murphy needed money for a payment, he was to direct an invoice "to me personally in Atlanta," Giles said, in an envelope marked "Personal." Once the check was made out and in his hands, Giles continued, he would mail it to Murphy, again in an envelope marked "Personal." These arrangements were made to "eliminate handling by any more people than was absolutely necessary," Giles said. Feldman executed the expanded contract, knowing what the $108,000 was for, and Leuty "was aware of the fact that I was making arrangements with Rowland Tompkins to handle these payments," Giles noted.

On September 20, the first of nine phone calls—made from the home of Roy Murphy in Paramus, New Jersey, or from a Rowland Tompkins' phone—was placed to 201/ME 4-2434, the number of Metro Motors in Woodbridge. At the end of October, Murphy mailed a phony work invoice to Atlanta for the initial payment of $20,000. Giles obtained a check in that amount and, after Feldman approved it, mailed it to Murphy who, in turn, gave it to Howard Tompkins. Tompkins gave it to his company's chief accountant with instructions to deposit it in the payroll account. Then, to get the cash he needed for the payment, Tompkins had a check drawn on that same account, but for $21,500, because, he said, "Normally when we draw payroll it is overdrawn in case of layoff and things like that."

The check for $21,500 was cashed on November 7, two days after Walter Zirpolo and Robert Jacks were re-elected on their "Tanks? No Tanks!" platform. On that same day, Tompkins told Murphy he had the cash. They went to Tompkins' home to count the money. He took off the bands that identified the bank from which the money came and counted it. Then, he said, "We put an elastic band around it so it wouldn't fly all over and it would be taken care of orderly, and put them in a yellow or brown envelope."

Still on the same day, November 7, the last of the nine phone calls was made to 201/ME 4-2434; and Murphy and Tompkins then drove from Briarcliff Manor to Woodbridge to deliver the $20,000 to Jacks, in keeping with an appointment made by Murphy. When they arrived, Murphy let Tompkins off at a diner. "I went in the diner and he left with the money and came back," Tompkins said. When Murphy got back he told Tompkins, "Mission accomplished."

Tompkins was in the hospital when the second payment, for $15,000, was to be made. And so he asked Ralph Bankes, his brother-in-law, to go through the "normal" procedure with the payroll account and accompany Murphy to Woodbridge to pay the money to Jacks. They made the trip on February 6, 1964. Murphy parked in front of the city hall, leaving the engine running. He went inside, Bankes said, but "came out almost right away and told me the Colonial man had the permit. It was now okay to deliver the money to Mr. Jacks." They drove to

Metro Motors. Leaving Bankes in the car, Murphy went in with the envelope containing the $15,000 which had been on the seat between them. "He came out," Bankes recalled, "and—well, his favorite saying was, 'Mission accomplished.' He said, 'Mission accomplished.'"

Before the final payment was made, however, a whole new situation arose.

At about the time the $15,000 payment was made, Colonial came to know with certainty that the pipe connecting the pipeline with the "tank farm" would have to be laid through five city-owned lots. Fred Stewart had drawings prepared, and then, on February 12, 1964, in a letter to Mayor Zirpolo, requested an appointment to open negotiations for easements. They met about three weeks later in Edison, New Jersey, where Zirpolo's Eastern Capital Corporation has offices in the Menlo Park Shopping Center. The receptionist asked him to wait while she went to see when the Mayor could see him. She opened the door to Zirpolo's office, and Stewart, still in the reception room, heard Zirpolo speaking. When she returned she said, "He will see you in a few minutes." But when Stewart was ushered into the office the Mayor had vanished. Instead, Robert Jacks was sitting behind his desk.

Stewart spread out his maps, but the Council president was impatient. "Yes, I know all about it," Jacks said. The Colonial official remembered how the conversation came quickly to the point:

. . . he says, "We have got to have some money in this thing." I said, "What are you talking about?" He said, "I am talking about a hundred thousand dollars. That's what I'm talking about." I says, "We just got through paying you fifty thousand." He said, "Yes, but we have got to have more this time." I says, "That sounds like extortion to me." He says, "I don't care what you call it. We got to have it before you will ever get your permit." That was it.

Stewart refolded his maps and left. "I went back down the turnpike and stopped at the first telephone I got to and called Atlanta," he said. He talked to his boss, L. P. Humann, who told him, "Have nothing more to do with it. Back off. Don't touch it any more." Stewart later said, "I followed his advice."

In Atlanta, Humann reported the demand for $100,000 to Glenn Giles, Colonial's vice-president for operations. Giles, in turn, passed the information on to Ben Leuty, and possibly also to Karl Feldman, who, in any event, became aware of it. "Mr. Leuty instructed me to drop it at that point and not have any further dealings in the matter until I heard something from him," Giles said.

In April, the following month, the National Municipal League and *Look* magazine honored Woodbridge as an "All America City." At about this time Henry Price, who reported on Woodbridge for the Perth Amboy newspaper, went by the Shell tract and saw that tanks were being erected. He was surprised, and he had good reason to be. The previous September, he had gone to the Forge Inn in Woodbridge to hear the Mayor talk at a Chamber of Commerce dinner. Zirpolo, then campaigning for re-election, had said he would make an announcement in the coming weeks about a new industry that was going to occupy the Shell tract.

After the talk, while driving the Mayor to City Hall,

Price had asked, "What about those twenty-two tanks? Is this the industry that you are going to announce?" Zirpolo had ridiculed the thought. "Republican hogwash," he had said. "There is no truth to that. They have no application in or anything like that." Zirpolo had been correct in saying that no application had been filed, but, of course, he had been withholding at least two pertinent facts: that on August 16, more than three weeks earlier, he had sent Fred Stewart to see Jacks, who had demanded $50,000 for a permit; and that the Mayor himself had instructed Colonial not to file for a permit until after the November election.

Later in September, when Price had pressed Zirpolo and Jacks about reports that a "tank farm" was to be built in Jacks's ward, the Council president had seen to it that Price was given a copy of the "Tanks? No Tanks!" flyer. The flyer, in a "P.S.," said of the reports, "Our opponents have spread this vicious lie about us." The Mayor, with Jacks agreeing, had said, "There is no tanks going in out there."

In October, Price recalled, Jacks, at a Council meeting, had assured a questioner that a public hearing would be held on any application that might be made to build on the Shell tract. On October 29, when the first Rowland Tompkins work invoice for the initial payment of $20,000 to the city officials was being processed in Atlanta, Price had attended a League of Women Voters meeting at which a candidate for the Council had charged that Jacks and Zirpolo were going to sneak tanks onto the tract. The two officials had been present, and once again there had been a denial, by Jacks.

But on a day in April 1964, right before Price's eyes,

the tanks were going up. Price drove to the city hall
where, in the building department, he found that Colonial
Pipeline had been issued a building permit on February 6.
Again, Price had good reason to be surprised. On the
eve of the day the permit was issued he had covered
a meeting of the Planning Board. He remembered that no
application from Colonial had been so much as discussed.
As a check on his memory, he looked up the Planning
Board minutes for the February 5 meeting. They made
no mention of Colonial Pipeline. The minutes book in
hand, Price confronted Jacks. The Council president could
not find an entry either, and went to consult the Mayor;
on returning, he agreed that no entry had been made.

Price, who wrote about all of this in the Perth Amboy
Evening News, asked Jacks what had happened to the
public hearing he had promised during the campaign. "We
don't consider this a controversial area," Jacks replied. A
day or two later, Price managed to interview the Mayor
about his denials during the campaign that Colonial was
going to build a "tank farm." Zirpolo said, "There was
no application at the time." Anyway, he added, the tanks
"will be a good asset to the community and they will be
landscaped properly, and no one will see them."

Sometime afterward, as if to correct an oversight, the
Planning Board minutes were amended to account for
the Colonial permit. The Mayor was a member of the
Board. Its chairman, Louis C. Cyktor, Jr., was a real-
estate man who, a few years earlier, had formed an equal
partnership with Zirpolo to buy a truck farm for $320,000.
They had thirty acres rezoned for garden apartments, called
New Amsterdam Village; and, as late as the fall of 1966,
they still owned the remaining seventy acres. Cyktor ex-

pected that eventually they would sell this land for development, making this a very successful investment for the
two of them.

Although Ben Leuty, president of Colonial Pipeline, left
Glenn Giles without further instructions about the demand
from Woodbridge for money, Giles undertook to bring up
the matter, on June 4, 1964, with an official of the Bechtel
Corporation. This firm, based in San Francisco, had the
contract to build the section of the pipeline north from
the Delaware River to Woodbridge. It has some 10,000
employees and annual revenues of about $750 million,
making it the largest engineering company in the world.
The Bechtel official with whom Giles spoke was Harry
F. Waste, a vice-president and manager of the pipeline
division. At the time, Waste was in Atlanta to try to
renegotiate its contract with Colonial, having encountered
various construction difficulties, changes in the course of
the pipeline, and other problems. "I had a very brief
conversation with Mr. Waste in reference to the situation
in Woodbridge," Giles said. "At that time I told him that
we may be running into a problem there and be calling
on him for some help." And, Giles added, he made the
nature of the "problem" clear. A few weeks later, on
July 6, the Bechtel contract was negotiated, upward, by
more than $1 million.

About three months went by. Then, in early October,
while Giles was in Colonial's construction office in Cherry
Hill, New Jersey, Ben Leuty phoned him from Atlanta.
"He informed me," Giles said, "that the amount of money
to be paid to the Woodbridge city officials was sixty thousand dollars and it was to be paid in three payments, and

asked me to make arrangements to get the money to pay them." How it happened that the demand from Woodbridge had been reduced by $40,000, Leuty didn't say, and Giles didn't ask.

"I called Harry Waste by telephone in California and told him that we were being— This money had been demanded of us, and asked him if he could assist us in making the payments," Giles said. "He told me he would check around among his company and see whether something of this nature could be handled, and get back in touch with me as soon as he could."

In San Francisco, Waste called in a subordinate, William L. Fallow, who had been with Bechtel for fourteen years and was manager of economics and planning in the pipeline division. Waste told Fallow of delays in the New Jersey job that, he said, were caused by the inability of Colonial to get its permits and easements on schedule. Recalling the conversation later, Fallow said Waste told him that Giles had asked for help, but did not explain why Colonial could not handle the matter itself. "When I told Mr. Waste that I would be glad to do what I could, he instructed me to travel to New Jersey," where, at the Colonial office in Cherry Hill, he would get instructions. "He told me there was a sum to be paid to Woodbridge in the amount of sixty thousand dollars," Fallow added. Fallow said he had experience in negotiating right-of-way permits but remarked, "I have never paid any amount for any permit."

On October 5, at the Cherry Hill office of Colonial, Fallow tried to find two men whose names Waste had given him, but, he said, no one there "knew me or what I was supposed to do." Fallow then went to his motel, the

Brunswick Inn in New Brunswick, and phoned Harry Waste, who was in Vancouver. Waste directed Fallow to phone Giles in Atlanta, which he did the next day. Giles told him that to fulfill an already negotiated agreement, Colonial had agreed to pay Woodbridge $60,000 in cash. "I asked him, would they not take a check?" Fallow said. "He said he didn't think they would, but I could try." Giles laughed when he said that, Fallow noted. Giles went on to tell him that the money was to be paid in three installments of $20,000 each—one immediately, the second when the easement was granted, and the third at a later date. Giles also gave Fallow the phone number of Robert Jacks, identifying him "as an assistant to the Mayor," and asked him to get in touch with him.

The same day, October 6, Fallow made an appointment to see Jacks, but at Mayor Zirpolo's private office in the Menlo Park Shopping Center. After they had agreed on dates on which the payments would be made, Fallow asked Jacks if he would accept checks. Jacks said no. Fallow then told him he would try to get the cash for the initial payment. He went to the Bechtel office in Edison, as Giles had suggested he do, to try to cash a check for $20,000, but a hard-nosed employee there refused to cooperate. Stuck, Fallow then phoned Waste, who was still in Vancouver, because "this seemed to be a very much different proposition than what I had originally understood from him." Waste, agreeing, advised Fallow to return to San Francisco, because now there was much that had to be clarified. The next day, Fallow went to see Jacks to tell him that he was leaving but would be back in about a week. "Fine, all right," Jacks said.

At Bechtel's office at 220 Brush Street, Fallow discussed

the situation with Waste, who meanwhile had come down from Vancouver. Later, in conversations with Waste and two other Bechtel vice-presidents, one of them the treasurer, Fallow was instructed to fly back to New Jersey. There, in the Bechtel field office in Edison, as had been arranged, he received the cash from Basil C. Licklider, then administrative manager for the firm's New York office. (Licklider, in turn, had been asked by a superior in San Francisco to get the money. "I asked him what it was for," Licklider said, "and he told me that it was for liquidated damages, for [a] right-of-way claim for the pipeline office." Licklider then had drawn a check for $20,000, cashed it at the Morgan Guaranty Trust Company, and drove over to Edison.)

With Licklider and Fallow in the Edison office was Robert L. Bowman, manager of construction for Bechtel's pipeline division. After the money was turned over, Bowman and Fallow went to Fallow's room at the Brunswick Inn. There, on the bed, they counted out the money—two hundred $100 bills. Fallow phoned Jacks to say he was ready to make the first installment. Jacks said to come over to Zirpolo's office in the shopping center at one o'clock. Bowman drove him there and waited in the car. Fallow went upstairs. Jacks greeted him and invited him to an inner office, a different one than he was in before.

"I gave him the cnvclope, the manila envelope containing the twenty thousand dollars," Fallow said. "He took the money out of the envelope and put it in a desk drawer. . . . I asked him if he wasn't going to count it. He said, 'No.'" Fallow did not ask for a receipt, believing there was not much possibility of getting one. He and Jacks agreed that Fallow would return with another $20,-

000 on November 2. Then he left, and Bowman drove him to the Brunswick Inn.

At the motel Fallow had a visit from Glenn Giles. "After the pleasantries," Fallow said, "he wanted to discuss how Bechtel would be reimbursed for the payments that it would be making to Woodbridge. He suggested that what Colonial would do would be to issue an extra work order in the amount of $120,000. I asked him, 'What do you mean, one hundred and twenty thousand dollars? Bechtel is paying Woodbridge sixty thousand.' He said, 'Well, Bechtel will need to pay income tax on the one hundred and twenty thousand,' and that would be roughly 50 percent of it, and that would leave sixty thousand to cover the payments to Woodbridge." According to Giles, Fallow then suggested that Bechtel could save Colonial the extra $60,000 by writing off the money, on its own records, as "liquidation of right-of-way damages in the City of Woodbridge." The first payment was in fact handled just that way. Cutting deeper into the cocoon of innocence Fallow had built around himself, Giles told Fallow about the payments for building permits being made by the Rowland Tompkins Corporation.

The second payment to Jacks was due on November 2. A few days before it was to be made, Stephen Bechtel, Jr., president and majority stockholder in the company bearing his name, learned from others in the organization of the $20,000 payment. He blew up. He told Harry Waste that unless Colonial at once provided a letter saying that it had authorized the payment and would reimburse his firm for it, he would fire three of his employees—apparently, Waste, Fallow and a collaborator in San Francisco. Waste then asked Giles to write such a letter; Giles did so, backdating it to October 6; but he later arranged to have the original returned to him, after which he destroyed it. Waste also called Fallow in and "told me that Bechtel was to have nothing further to do with the Woodbridge matter and that I was to forget all about it," Fallow said. In the Bechtel firm, big as it was, ownership was not separated from management in the way it is in most corporations, including Colonial Pipeline. So Stephen Bechtel's personal ethics could show, and they did. But with Bechtel determined to keep his company out, how could the remaining two payments be made?

For reasons that are not fully clear, Robert Bowman, Bechtel's manager of pipeline construction, who was working with Giles on the pipeline and had helped Fallow count out the two hundred $100 bills for the first payment, nevertheless remained in the picture. First he called Giles. He "indicated to me," Giles said, "that other arrangements would have to be made, that Bechtel would no longer handle it in this matter." On November 18, more than two weeks after the second payment was due, Bowman had lunch at the Brunswick Inn with Robert S. Gates, president of the Gates Construction and Gates Equipment Corporations, of Little Ferry, New Jersey. These firms, under a subcontract from Bechtel, had built the Raritan River crossing of the line. During lunch, without saying why, Bowman said that the Bechtel company needed $20,000 in a hurry and asked Gates if he could raise it.

"I very readily said yes," Gates recalled. ". . . ten years previous Bechtel had helped me when I was in a bind for a payroll on a job crossing the Hudson River. They advanced me the money to meet my payroll." After Gates had said he would provide the $20,000, Bowman said that an additional $20,000 would be needed later on, and Gates agreed to provide that, too.

"He said that we would make an 'extra' out of the Raritan River crossing," Gates said. "During the course of crossing the river, we encountered a large amount of rock which slowed us down considerably. However, the rock was part of our contract, and Mr. Bowman suggested that this would make a good 'extra' to raise the capital we needed." The next day, at Gate's office, they agreed that Bechtel would give Gates $84,800, the additional $44,800 being the "hypothetical" sum computed by Gates's bookkeeper to be necessary for Federal taxes, state taxes and insurance. Then they wrote up phony orders for the "extra" work.

The day after that, November 20, after Glenn Giles flew up from Atlanta, he and Bowman lunched at the Brunswick Inn. Giles approved the arrangements, which obligated Colonial to pick up the tab for the $84,800 through billings by Bechtel under a cost-plus contract. Then, to prepare for transmitting the second $20,000 payment, Gates wrote seven checks. Each was for less than $5000, the "trigger" amount for many IRS inquiries. One check was to cash, one to himself and five to trusted employees whom he asked to "deliver me back the cash." In this way Gates accumulated $20,000 in ten- and twenty-dollar bills by November 24.

On that day, he said, "I wrapped it up in newspapers . . . and I carried it down to the Brunswick Inn where Mr. Bowman had an appointment to meet me. . . . I gave it to Mr. Bowman, and he counted it out on the bed." In exchange for the $20,000, Bowman gave Gates a Bechtel check for $42,400, the sum that would enable Gates to break even. Bowman put the cash in an envelope and the envelope in his briefcase. Then he and Gates had lunch. "He asked me if I would go over and deliver the money with him, and I said sure," Gates said. Bowman did not identify the prospective recipient. They drove to the Menlo Park Shopping Center, where "Mr. Bowman introduced me to a Mr. Jacks":

> . . . he asked me what business I was in. I told him the construction business, and he told me he was in the automobile business. He gave me his card and told me if I was buying any automobiles or something like that to look him up, and then we gave the money to him, put the money on the table, to the best of my knowledge, and Bowman had his briefcase and handed me the envelope and instructed me to give it to Mr. Jacks. I put it on the table . . . He shoved it into a drawer and it wasn't discussed at all, as best I can remember.

The two men then left. "I made some crack to Bob [Bowman], wasn't he going to count it or something, but Bob passed it off and he said in about three weeks or so he would need the other twenty thousand dollars and for me to get it together in small amounts, which I did," Gates said.

Three days later, on November 27, a certificate of occupancy having been issued for the "tank farm," Rowland Tompkins executives Howard Tompkins and Ralph Bankes counted out $15,000 in cash, as had been done before. Then they drove from Briarcliff Manor, New York, to Edison, New Jersey. There, in the Menlo Park Shopping Center, Tompkins waited in the car while Bankes delivered the final payment for the building permit to Jacks. The transaction took place in one of Mayor Zirpolo's two private offices there. "A nice office," Bankes remarked to Jacks. Of the aggregate of six payments, totaling $110,000, only the last remained to be made. To get ready for it, Robert Gates, following instructions from Robert Bowman of the Bechtel Corporation, assembled $20,000, again in small bills. "I paid my brother a bonus, and I paid myself a bonus, and I instructed my brother to take out the money in cash . . . and give it to me, and I did the same thing, and we wound back up with twenty thousand dollars," Gates said. On December 14, he and Bowman met, as before, at the Brunswick Inn, and counted out the money on Bowman's bed. Bowman gave Gates a Colonial Pipeline check for $42,400, in exchange for the $20,000 in cash. They lunched. With the cash in an envelope in Bowman's briefcase, they drove to the Menlo Park Shopping Center and were ushered in to see Bob Jacks. "This time," Gates said, "we didn't spend any time or much conversation, left the envelope on the table and out we went."

In 1965, without competitive bidding, Colonial awarded a maintenance contract for the pipeline to the Gates Equipment and Gates Construction Corporations. Also in 1965, Ben Leuty, Colonial's president, was promoted to vice-chairman of the board of directors.

The time came, in May 1966, when FBI agents happened upon, and were struck by, the canceled check for the first $20,000 payment, but it was by the sheerest chance.

As early as 1961, Louis H. Woiwode and Edwin Dooley,

both of the Office of Labor-Management and Welfare-Pension Reports of the Department of Labor, discovered that embezzlement of union funds contributed by pipeline workers was occurring on a wholesale basis. The workers were vulnerable, because as a pipeline was built they moved from the jurisdiction of one union local to another. On entering a new jurisdiction they were required, so long as they stayed there, to pay temporary dues called "dobies." This was done through a payroll "check-off," or directly. Woiwode, as director of the Detroit office, authorized several investigations. These established that business agents for some locals of the International Union of Operating Engineers and the Laborers' International Union, both AFL-CIO, simply pocketed the "dobies."

In August 1964, after several successful prosecutions in the Detroit area, the Labor Department began an enlarged investigation. Richard Gump, president of the National Pipeline Association, spoke with Dooley about the Colonial project, then nearing completion, and listed among its contractors the Osage Construction Company of Tulsa, Oklahoma. But, Dooley said later, when he went to Osage he was told that Osage had not been permitted to work on the pipeline because Peter W. Weber, president of a local of the Operating Engineers with jurisdiction throughout New Jersey (and, as well, five counties in southern New York State), "had forced Colonial and Osage to withdraw from its construction contract."

Karl Feldman, executive vice-president of Colonial, and Glenn Giles, manager of construction, confirmed this to Dooley at Colonial headquarters in Atlanta. They said that Colonial, at substantially higher cost, had been forced to replace Osage with another contractor having friendly relations with Peter Weber, and that the Bechtel Corporation, the prime contractor, had been forced to employ nonworking union agents and stewards. "Mr. Feldman demanded an investigation by the Government," Dooley said.

Early in 1965, in San Francisco, Anthony B. Cosola, a Labor Department investigator examining Bechtel's records, found evidence of how bad the labor situation was: Several union stewards claimed to have worked, and were paid for, a succession of 126-hour weeks. Purportedly, they had worked twenty-one hours a day, six days a week. They had contrived to be paid even when labor troubles shut down the job completely. In less than twelve months' actual construction time, each of these stewards had managed to gross more than $50,000.

Woiwode, the Labor Department official in Detroit, saw in the whole matter a clear pattern of extortion, an offense that lies entirely within Justice Department jurisdiction. On March 22, 1965, accordingly, he referred the case to the Organized Crime and Racketeering Section of the Justice Department. The FBI then undertook a seven-month investigation. The Department followed up by authorizing a further investigation by a special grand jury. Attorney General Ramscy Clark appointed three young special attorneys—Philip T. White, 38; Herbert J. Stern, 32; and Jonathan L. Goldstein, 28—to lead the investigation. They convened the grand jury in February, 1966, in Newark, New Jersey. Promptly, the grand jury began to subpoena witnesses and records and to hear testimony.

In May, examining subpoenaed records at the Bechtel Corporation, an FBI agent who has not been publicly identified came on a $20,000 check that was suspect because it had been negotiated for cash. Large corporations ordinarily don't write checks of such size for cash. The check was one that Basil Licklider had cashed at Morgan Guaranty Trust in October, 1964, into the two hundred $100 bills that William Fallow had then delivered to Robert Jacks.

The grand jury, knowing none of this background, subpoenaed Licklider to appear before it on June 1, 1966. His lawyers, also representing Bechtel, requested he be excused. The Justice Department denied the request. Then, on May 31, Bechtel's lawyers started to open the door of a closet filled with skeletons. At a meeting with Special Attorneys Stern and Goldstein, the latter said, the company lawyers revealed that the Bechtel Corporation

> had assisted in paying $60,000 in cash, in three equal payments, to the Mayor and President of the Town Council of Woodbridge, New Jersey. Specifically, they informed us that Bechtel, and its employees, had made these three $20,000 payments in cash, which was later reimbursed by Colonial, and that the check, originally discovered by the FBI, had been issued to obtain the cash for the first payment. The attorneys for Bechtel stated that it was the desire of their clients to cooperate in the investigation, and that they wished an adjournment of Licklider's subpoena so that they could complete their own investigation.
>
> Moreover, they stated that they needed this additional time to contact the Colonial attorneys in order to ascertain, from Colonial, why Colonial had initially authorized this transaction, a transaction in which Bechtel had acted merely as delivery agent. Pursuant

to these requests, the subpoena . . . was vacated by Mr. Stern and myself.

On June 6, 1966, the attorneys for Bechtel . . . informed us that Colonial had absolutely refused to come forward with any information, and that they were, therefore, in no position to say just what had caused Colonial to make this payment through Bechtel; except that this $60,000 had apparently been paid for certain payments and easements.

Over the next several days, Stern and Goldstein, taking up Bechtel's offer to cooperate, brought Fallow and Licklider before the grand jury. The prosecutors also served a subpoena on Glenn Giles for Colonial's records. He brought them before the grand jury on June 8 and, notably, revoked the waiver of immunity from prosecution that he had routinely signed earlier, when he appeared to testify in the Peter Weber case. No questions were asked of him.

On June 15, the prosecutors met, at his initiative, with David T. Wilentz, of Perth Amboy, the Democratic National Committeeman from New Jersey but even better known as the State Attorney General who had prosecuted Bruno Richard Hauptmann in the Lindbergh kidnaping case. Wilentz came to Newark, however, in his capacity as a partner in Wilentz, Goldman & Spitzer, which was representing Colonial Pipeline. Wilentz said he understood the company still did not wish to enlighten the Government. The next day, a subpoena went out for those Colonial records that might show what had caused the firm to pay $60,000 to the elected leaders of Woodbridge. On June 22, the day before the records were to be produced, Wilentz surprised Special Attorneys Stern and Goldstein with a revelation: Colonial had given Zirpolo and Jacks not merely the $60,000 known to the Government, but earlier, through the Rowland Tompkins Corporation, an additional $50,-000.

Wilentz, by volunteering this information rather than awaiting its inevitable discovery by the Government, in the subpoenaed records, laid groundwork for a claim that Colonial had been not the perpetrator of the crime of bribery, but the victim of the crime of extortion, albeit extortion that it had never reported, or seriously thought of reporting, to any law-enforcement agency. Given a few days to assemble supporting evidence, Wilentz claimed, he could demonstrate the truth of his argument.

On June 29, Wilentz, accompanied by Glenn Giles and Fred Stewart, the Colonial rights-of-way buyer for New Jersey, returned to see Stern and Goldstein. That day and the next, the prosecutors interviewed the Colonial officials. They ended up persuaded that the top echelon of Colonial, Ben Leuty and Karl Feldman, had the final responsibility "for authorizing and ordering" the payments. Moreover, Goldstein said later, "it appeared that Leuty himself had conducted negotiations" with the Mayor and the Council president to reduce by $40,000 the original solicitation for the rights-of-way through the city-owned lots. Consequently, Goldstein said, Stern and he "determined . . . that a complaint of extortion could not be established or resolved without exploring the intent of these men, and means by which they had been able to convert a solicitation for one hundred thousand dollars into an actual payment of sixty thousand."

During July, Fred Stewart testified before the grand jury, Wilentz having requested that he be subpoenaed.

Giles, however, testified voluntarily. After answering questions, he accepted an invitation from the grand jury to make any comments he cared to in his own way. "I know what we did was wrong and immoral and unethical," he said. Not once did he use a word such as "extortion," "hold-up," or "shakedown."

Wilentz requested that subpoenas be issued, too, for Leuty and Feldman, but then, saying they would appear voluntarily, asked that they be vacated. Feldman came first, on July 1, the same day as Giles. That part of the transcript of the proceeding that is public shows Feldman offering to tell the jurors

> why people get into a situation like this. I wondered myself sometimes. Several of us were sacrificed personally to get this job done and we were faced with the task of trying to get it done and this is the only way we could see to get the job done. That's all I have to say.

Leuty testified on July 13, and, again, only an incomplete stenographic record is public. At one point, Special Attorney Goldstein asked, "Is there anything that you want to add?" and Leuty responded:

> Well, I'm not much of a talker . . . but the Defense Department had talked to one of the directors and they had wished that this line could be done about the time of the Cuban crisis because it does give the means of handling all sorts of products from the Gulf Coast refinery area to the New York Harbor area. It is strictly not at the advantage of submarines. In fact, we made monthly reports of our construc-

tion progress to someone in the Defense Department to let them know how far we were along. I will admit this didn't get done in time for the Cuban crisis but we didn't know when the crisis would be over and we were doing our dead-level best to get this done in time for that and then . . . the second demand came up. [The Cuban crisis—the installation of Soviet missiles in Cuba, and its aftermath—flared and ended in October 1962. It was at that very period that Colonial spent five or six weeks checking on whether Shell Oil had a clear title to the Woodbridge tract. The target date for finishing the pipeline, January 1964, was exceeded by more than a year. The "second demand"—for $100,000—was made in March 1964.]

After Goldstein noted that the Cuban crisis had ended before the "second demand," Leuty testified that another crisis could occur and, in that event, fortunately, the pipeline is in place "and is free from submarines coming up the coast."

Such were the explanations of Colonial officials, offered voluntarily, as to why they had ordered the payment of $110,000 to the Woodbridge officials. Such explanation as Leuty may have offered as to the 40 percent discount on the demand for $100,000, is not in the public record. Yet, all things considered, the circumstances would seem to have been about as favorable as could be hoped to persuade the grand jury that Colonial and its executives were innocent of bribery.

On February 23, 1967, an unpersuaded grand jury returned an indictment. It contained two conspiracy counts

—one for use of interstate facilities (the mails, phones, airlines, highways) to get the building permit by bribery, the other to use the communications and travel facilities to get the easements. There were also seven substantive counts, each involving a trip across state lines to deliver cash for the permits or the easements. All nine counts named Colonial Pipeline, Leuty, Feldman, Giles, and the Woodbridge officials, Zirpolo and Jacks. Three substantive counts named the Rowland Tompkins and Gates Equipment firms, and two each named the Bechtel and Gates Construction companies. In addition, the indictment listed as nonindicted coconspirators: Robert Gates, Howard Tompkins and Ralph Bankes, the brothers-in-law; and Robert Bowman, William Fallow, and Harry Waste, the Bechtel trio.

For more than a year after the indictment was returned there were motions to dismiss and other pretrial matters that were disposed of. Then, in October 1968, the Government made a critical move: It severed Glenn Giles from the other defendants, in hopes he would testify against them. Giles not only refused to do this, but also invoked the Fifth Amendment against self-incrimination. However, Ramsey Clark, the Attorney General, overcame this when he requested, in a letter, that Giles be exempted from prosecution. Special Attorney Stern then presented the letter to the judge handling the case, Reynier J. Wortendyke, Jr. With that, Wortendyke ordered Giles to testify at the trial. A couple of weeks later, the Gates Equipment and Gates Construction companies each retracted pleas of innocent and pleaded guilty to one indictment count. The trial of the remaining defendants began the next day, November 13, 1968.

The defense attorneys arrayed for the trial were, by most

any standard, prestigious. The principal lawyer for Colonial Pipeline was Warren W. Wilentz, son of the Democratic National Committeeman and, until just a few days before the trial opened, Democratic aspirant for the United States Senate seat held by Clifford P. Case. Ben Leuty's chief counsel was Simon Rifkind, the former Federal judge. He was a senior partner in Paul, Weiss, Goldberg, Rifkind, Wharton & Garrison, a famous New York City law firm whose other partners included Arthur J. Goldberg, former Associate Justice of the Supreme Court of the United States, Ramsey Clark, former Attorney General, and Theodore C. Sorensen, a top aide to the late President Kennedy. Edward Bennett Williams, of Washington, the widely known criminal lawyer, represented Mayor Zirpolo. Joseph E. Brill, attorney for Roy Cohn, the entrepreneur who had been one of the boy wonders in the retinue of the late Senator Joseph R. McCarthy, represented the Rowland Tompkins Corporation. John E. Toolan, a former New Jersey State Senator, represented Robert Jacks. The counsel for the Bechtel Corporation was Frederick B. Lacey, who went on to become the United States Attorney for New Jersey and, after that, a Federal judge in Newark.

Reynier Wortendyke, the trial judge, was seventy-three, an appointee of President Eisenhower; he was alert, expert, decisive, impatient with irrelevancy, tough and fair. The trial proceeded reasonably predictably, with one major exception. On December 1, Mayor Zirpolo was stricken at his home by heart disease; later, with the agreement of the Government, he was severed from the trial. As to the rest of the trial, the points to be noted include these:

Leuty and Feldman did not take the stand; neither did

the Woodbridge officials. Giles, who had told the grand
jury, "I knew what we did was wrong," had been promoted
to a vice-presidency at Colonial by the time of the trial; and
with his trial testimony he tried to exonerate not only Leuty
and Feldman, but also Zirpolo and Jacks. Before the
grand jury Giles had said that Feldman knew about the
transactions growing out of the "second demand"; but
before the trial jury he corrected that testimony. Before
the grand jury Giles had sworn that he was told that
if the first demand, for $50,000, was met, the Woodbridge
officials would "jam through" the building permits over
the residents' objections; but before the trial jury he spoke
of the news being greeted with howls of righteous indignation. (Feldman had "pounded the table," Leuty had been
"agitated," and he, Giles, had exclaimed, "The dirty bastards are shaking us down.") Out of the presence of the
jury, Herbert Stern, who tried the case for the Government,
said of Giles, "I assume that he expects when he finishes
testifying to go back and continue to be vice-president of
Colonial."

There was at least one humorous moment. Stern took
William Fallow through two step-by-step reviews of the
episode in which he got $20,000 in small bills from Basil
Licklider, his fellow Bechtel employee, counted it out on
a motel bed, went to the Menlo Park Shopping Center, and
gave the cash to Robert Jacks, without asking for a receipt.

"Mr. Fallow," Stern then asked, "is it still your testimony
that the twenty thousand dollars was going into the Woodbridge treasury?"

"Yes, sir," Fallow replied.

A final point about the trial was the clarity with which
it established the way certain things are done. When pay-

ments for the building permits were made, Roy Murphy, an employee of Rowland Tompkins, handed over the cash, while Ralph Bankes, a vice-president, remained in the car; when Murphy was ill, Howard Tompkins, who was to become president, stayed in the car while Bankes carried the cash to Jacks. Colonial put the arm on the Bechtel Corporation, its contractor, until Stephen Bechtel found out about it; then the money-passing chore went down the ladder, to a much smaller outfit, the Gates companies. Starting with Ben Leuty at Colonial, prosecutor Stern pointed out, each person involved "passed a dirty job down to the next one because each one knew that what they were doing was unlawful."

Defense counsel made closing arguments to the jury on January 14 and 15, 1969. For the Bechtel company, Frederick Lacey said the facts "reflect a composite of a corporation that is not . . . venal." For Ben Leuty, then and at a later proceeding, Simon Rifkind depicted "the commander-in-chief of the greatest pipeline ever built anywheres in the whole wide world" as the victim of a crime. In trying to get the job done Leuty, who by now was retired, had been a patriot: "What the submarines did to those tankers you all remember from your own knowledge of what happened in World War II." Yes, nine oil companies owned Colonial, but they, in turn, were owned by "more than one million stockholders, men, women, children, widows, orphans, of every kind of character." Leuty is a man of "superlative qualities of character as a law-abiding citizen, as a moral citizen."

When Leuty was apprised of the demand for $50,000, he had to make "one of the gravest decisions . . . in his whole life," Rifkind continued. Apart from Colonial, what would a delay do to the contractors? The oil companies waiting to send through the pipeline enough oil to fill eighty thousand fuel trucks? What of the interest charge, which "for every day's delay is forty thousand dollars?" Leuty authorized the payments to Jacks because "he and his company were threatened with massive injury amounting to a national disaster . . . He capitulated to a force and fear beyond his capacity to resist." Further, "all of the evidence showed conclusively that what Leuty and his people tried to do was to prevent the officials of Woodbridge from acting dishonestly and illegally. . . .

"Yours will be the glory," Rifkind told the jury toward the end of his closing argument, "when you wipe the tear off his lovely wife's cheek."

Adrian M. Foley, speaking for Feldman, thanked Rifkind for generously including his client, whenever it was appropriate, in furnishing the defense of Leuty. Then he argued that not only was Feldman "a victim and not a transgressor, but he was equally as well a victim of . . . a tortured, illogical and unreasonable attempt to make the facts fit into a preconceived, precast mold, and a mold which fell apart when it was tested by trial."

Warren Wilentz, for Colonial, said, "There is no real fight about the facts in this case. The real question is the intent." All of the proof offered by the prosecution, he said, "is that it was a shakedown, that it was coercion, that it was duress and that these men did not have any intention and this corporation no intention to commit bribery. It intended not to commit a crime." Joseph Brill, defending Rowland Tompkins, argued that Howard Tompkins, Ralph Bankes and Roy Murphy (who had died not long after the episode) had performed a check-cashing service, a courtesy by which Colonial was enabled to transmit cash to an official of Woodbridge.

"I am going to talk for a minute about campaign contributions and cash, and maybe it will be a shock to some of you folks," former State Senator Toolan said in behalf of Robert Jacks.

> I don't know whether any of you has had any political exposure at all to talk in terms of cash. How do you think political campaigns are run? Did you every try to hire a poll worker or a car or get a babysitter for somebody to go out to vote, and think you can pay them with a check on Election Day?
>
> Members of the jury, elections in this nation are run with cash in every municipality, in every county, and everywhere along the line. . . . you just have to realize that political money is cash money. . . . Every political party must have somebody in it who has the capacity to raise money. . . . Bob Jacks was that person in the Woodbridge political organization. . . . Now, this is an oil company coming through. He had to raise money either by going around and sandbagging local people, or you get it on a one-shot deal with some big asset that is coming through, and you take advantage of it.

The final summation was that of Herbert Stern, the prosecutor. He reviewed the indictment and the law; marshaled the facts and the evidence for the Government; quoted verbatim excerpts of trial testimony; attacked claims that the defendants were waging antisubmarine warfare, cashing checks as a courtesy or engaging in political fund-raising; and, "on behalf of the United States," professed not "the slightest fear that you will do your duty to all parties." But the memorable passage was this one:

> Ladies and gentlemen, rarely if ever has the United States been able to pull back the curtain and to display before you or any jury the kind of naked corruption that we have displayed in this case, the intimate details to corrupt public officials met and joined, furthered and promoted by big businessmen who were equally corrupt for their own reasons. Ladies and gentlemen, I suggest to you that rarely if ever has the United States been able to prove such a deliberate, knowing, intentional and willful flouting of the laws of the United States. . . .
>
> Ladies and gentlemen, these cases are rare indeed, and they are not easy to come by, and they do make history when they do come. . . . Let me suggest to you the reason that these cases are so rare is because the men don't often get caught. . . . Does it stretch your imagination or offend your common sense when I suggest to you the reason they don't get caught is because generally they hide it too well, and if you doubt it, ladies and gentlemen, look how well it was hidden in this case.

In instructing the jury, Judge Wortendyke had to deal with the crucial issue of whether the crime was bribery, as asserted by the Government, or extortion, as asserted by counsel for Colonial and its executives. Simon Rifkind, in his opening and again in his summary arguments for Ben Leuty, had used a simile in which the executive was "not a predatory dog but a sheep that yielded a piece of its hide in order to escape with its fleece." On both occasions, he also told of a visitor to an art gallery who sees a painting that prompts him to ask, "Is that a picture of a sunrise or a sunset?" Superficially, he told the jury, a sunset and a sunrise "look so much alike. One marks the decline of the day, the onset of darkness and cold; the other, the sunrise, heralds a new dawn, the blossoming of a new day bright with the life of new adventure and renewed life.

"Now, ladies and gentlemen," Rifkind continued, "you have inspected that picture. You have inspected it for eight long weeks. You have heard the story. . . . Are you not prepared to agree with me that in looking at the picture of Ben Leuty as it was developed on that witness stand, you saw not a criminal but a victim of the crime?"

But Herbert Stern, in the prosecution summation, suggested that the jurors need not worry whether they were seeing a sunrise or a sunset. ". . . you are going to be surprised," he said. ". . . you are going to find out from the Judge that the law of bribery is just what you always thought it was . . ."

Three days later, on Monday, January 20, Judge Wortendyke instructed the jury as the prosecutor predicted he would. Under New Jersey law, the Judge said, bribery of a public official occurs not only when he accepts, but when he is *offered,* an undue reward with the corrupt intent of influencing his behavior in office and inclining him to act contrary to the accepted rules of honesty and integrity. Once the mere offer is made, that is, the crime of bribery is committed; thus extortion, even if it occurs, is not a defense to bribery.

At 4 P.M. on January 23, the jurors—eight men and four women—returned to the courtroom. "The Clerk may interrogate the jury as to its verdicts," the Judge said. The jury had convicted all of the defendants: Colonial, on all nine counts; Leuty, Feldman, and Jacks, on the two conspiracy counts; Rowland Tompkins, on the building-permit conspiracy count; and the Bechtel Corporation, on the easements conspiracy count; Rowland Tompkins, on four substantive counts; and Bechtel and Jacks, on one such count each.

The sentencing lay months ahead. Meanwhile, the three young Special Attorneys—Herbert Stern, Jonathan Goldstein, and Philip White—prosecuted the labor case that grew out of the very same ninety-mile stretch of pipeline in New Jersey. On June 7, 1969, a jury in Judge Wortendyke's court convicted Peter Weber of conspiring to extort a $300,000 subcontract from the Bechtel Corporation for the Joyce Pipeline Company of Andover, New York; of the extortion itself, and of receiving three payments of $3500 each from the H. C. Price Company, a contracting firm in Bartlesville, Oklahoma.[2]

Before the main sentencing proceeding in the Colonial case got under way in late June, Judge Wortendyke was able to dispose of the sentencing of the Gates Construction

---

[2] Wortendyke later sentenced Weber to ten years in prison and fined him $30,000. The Court of Appeals for the Third Circuit rebuffed an appeal. Weber was then sixty-one and an international vice-president of the Operating Engineers, as well as president and business manager of a local, No. 825, with 6400 members.

James V. Joyce, president of the firm bearing his name, having paid Weber $30,000, or 10 percent of the face amount of the subcontract, was indicted along with Weber, became a star witness against him, was himself convicted of a violation of the Taft-Hartley Act, and was fined $1000.

and Gates Equipment firms. On their pleas of guilty, the Judge fined them $2500 each. He said these "light" sentences were in order because Robert Gates had testified for the Government and "fully cooperated with the Court."

In the main proceeding, counsel for the individual defendants pleaded that their clients not be imprisoned. In behalf of Robert Jacks, John Toolan said his client had borne the burden of "humiliation and disgrace without whimpering"; he told of his war record and his family. For Ben Leuty, Simon Rifkind said that the Colonial executive had "committed a grave error when he failed to discern where the true path of responsibility lay, and because he made this mistake he stands before you today labeled a felon." One of the three major purposes of criminal judgments is retribution, but has not Ben Leuty, "in the context of his prior experience . . . already been punished and lashed and flagellated far more intensely and far more cruelly than any punishment which this civilized court would . . . administer?" Rehabilitation is a second purpose of a criminal judgment—but this word is hardly appropriate for a man whose entire life has been a model "of what adherence to Christian morality produces." As to the third purpose, deterrence, of what relevance is this to a man whose friends, those who wrote to the Judge to plead for mercy, know "how he resisted every temptation, clung to the faith of his fathers, served his neighbors well, faithfully discharged every trust committed to him?" Similarly, Adrian Foley, pleading for Karl Feldman, asked the Judge to "see how great his shame, how great his contribution, and how great his suffering," all of which resulted from the "indiscretion" of "lending his name, countersigning things thrust before him."

Warren Wilentz spoke briefly for Colonial Pipeline, which, Judge Wortendyke noted from the company's balance sheet before him, had total assets as of December 31, 1968, of $385,000,199. Wilentz said, "I know I represent a corporation, and rather a young corporation, if Your Honor please, which I am afraid lost its way. It was organized to build a pipeline from Texas to New Jersey and got lost around Woodbridge, sadly enough."

Judge Wortendyke, before passing sentence, said,

> Well, I have something to say about this entire case. It was a liberal education to me of the amorality of business, politics and human relations in this democracy of ours. . . . I may be a little old-fashioned and a bit narrow in my views, but I was astounded when I looked into the faces of the individual defendants and heard about the corporate defendants in this case, and as I have further learned from the very complete presentence report, that such a thing could have transpired. I cannot yet understand why a corporation such as the Colonial Pipeline Company would pay any money.
>
> Oh, yes, they were cognizant of delays and all that sort of thing, that they were in business [but] . . . their conduct of the other corporations . . . shakes my faith in business in this country.

The Judge imposed the maximum allowable penalty of $10,000 per count on the three corporate defendants, for a total of $70,000. Leuty, Feldman and Jacks faced possible prison sentences of up to five years per count. "If you had committed a crime of violence," the Judge told Jacks, "I would have given you a maximum period of imprisonment because I have no patience with it." Instead, however, Wortendyke imposed on each of the three men suspended sentences of a year and a day, and he put them on unsupervised probation for five years.

The defendants petitioned for a new trial. This failing, they appealed to the United States Court of Appeals for the Third Circuit. While the appeals were pending, one noteworthy event occurred.[3] Mayor Walter Zirpolo, having recuperated from the heart disease that had caused him to be severed from his codefendants, went to trial before Judge Wortendyke and was convicted. But, on the ground that the prosecutor, Special Attorney Frank Kiernan, had made a reversible error during the proceeding, the Judge granted a motion for a new trial.

The whole dismaying affair came to a bizarre ending. The defendants (other than Zirpolo), in seeking a reversal of their convictions, asserted numerous grounds for doing so, as would be expected in a major case in which highly skilled counsel seeks out and exploits every possibility of error in prolonged pretrial and trial procedures. One of their claims had to do with the special grand jury that returned the indictment in February 1967, a year after it was sworn. There were twenty-three grand jurors, of whom

[3] Actually, there was one other noteworthy occurrence. Frederick Lacey, who had represented the Bechtel Corporation, was made United States Attorney for New Jersey. Lacey then named Herbert Stern, his courtroom adversary, as his chief assistant and Jonathan Goldstein, Stern's fellow prosecutor, as Chief of the Criminal Division. This team launched an unprecedented series of prosecutions for corruption in public office in New Jersey. After Lacey was named to the Federal Bench, Stern became U. S. Attorney, and he and Goldstein continued the prosecutions.

five were women: two "homemakers," a housewife, a switchboard operator, and a stock girl.

About three months after this special grand jury returned its indictment, a member of the Wilentz law firm in Perth Amboy, acting for all defense counsel except for those representing the two Woodbridge officials, investigated the process by which the grand jury was impaneled. For at least a quarter-century, the attorney said, the practice in selecting prospective grand jurors had been to choose at least two men for every woman, even though women comprise 52.2 percent of the adult population of New Jersey. Thus, defense counsel argued, the indictment was invalid because the grand jury that voted it had been impaneled by a method that inflicted "systematic and deliberate discrimination against women."

On February 18, 1971, in Philadelphia, the Court of Appeals agreed. "The judgments of conviction will be reversed," it said.

AUTHOR'S NOTE: This chapter was constructed, with very few and trivial exceptions, from a review of several thousand pages of trial transcript, court exhibits and pre- and posttrial proceedings. The direct quotations, including those of Henry Price, the newspaper reporter, and the excerpts from grand jury testimony, are all from these public sources. In addition, I reported the Colonial and Peter Weber cases for the Washington *Post*.

CHAPTER FOUR

"Get Away With What You Can"

by SANFORD J. UNGAR

THE pharmaceutical industry of the United States is very
big business. Its magazine advertisements and television
commercials emphasize its selfless scientific research, its
unrelenting humanitarian concern for healing the sick, and
its zeal in producing efficient, effective drugs at minimal
cost. But it has another, less noble aspect. For it is an
industry of intense competition and almost limitless profits,
populated by industrial scientists whose first concern seldom is science but rather the dollar; by doctors who have
not been near a patient or a laboratory for years; by promoters, salesmen and other pitchmen—all presided over by
corporate executives many of whom care little whether

they are producing pills or pegboards so long as the money rolls in and keeps the stockholders happy. A new drug that is promptly approved by the Federal Government and zestfully promoted by a company can mean an extraordinary bonanza. The stakes are high, and some pharmaceutical companies lose on a few of their gambles; but if a company can promise a cure and give the appearance of actually providing it in at least a few carefully publicized cases, the prospects for success are superb. Sometimes success comes easily. Sometimes it must be helped along.

One of the biggest and most successful of the American drug companies is Richardson-Merrell, Inc. A conglomerate which until 1960 was called the Vick Chemical Company, it hovers around number 300 on *Fortune* magazine's list of the 500 largest industrial corporations in the United States. It provides the public with a wide variety of products, from nostrums like Vicks Vaporub to medicines of great sophistication.

Much of the corporation's most important work is done by a major subsidiary in Cincinnati, the William S. Merrell Company, in a plant with the latest in modern laboratory facilities. The Cincinnati operation is customarily headed by some of the parent corporation's top men, and these men are entrenched in the elite of that city's business community. They and their colleagues at Procter & Gamble and other large firms take pride in having made Cincinnati one of the most prosperous cities of the Middle West. Cincinnati is proud of Merrell, too. Some of the research conducted there is reported in the local newspapers and is often a topic of conversation.

In the late 1950s and early 1960s, the talk was about

a new Merrell drug called MER/29, to be used in treating heart disease. Apart from what it might do medically, Merrell executives looked to MER/29 for a major corporate shot in the arm, a success which could reinforce the firm's strong position in the pharmaceutical industry and bring in money to finance plans to expand.

News of MER/29, one of a number of compounds falling under the generic name of triparanol, was greeted eagerly by heart patients in the late 1950s. Medical research had convinced a substantial number of respected authorities that high levels of cholesterol, a fatlike substance in blood and tissue, were a contributing factor in hardening of the arteries and thus one of the major causes of heart attacks. After several years of developing MER/29, Merrell patented its formula for the drug, which, the company said, seemed to reduce cholesterol or inhibit its formation in monkeys and other lower animals. It would cost only thirty-five cents per capsule and could be adopted as part of a heart patient's therapy with hardly any change in diet. The odds were excellent that Merrell would reap great medical and financial bounties from the new drug.

In mid-1958, the company distributed a "very preliminary confidential brochure" suggesting that doctors try MER/29 on their private patients and report the results. About a year later, in July 1959, Merrell filed a standard new drug application with the Food and Drug Administration. At that time, long before the consumer movement had begun to play watchdog on Federal agencies and programs, to obtain approval for marketing a new drug a company had to prove only that it was safe for laboratory animals and that it had no serious side effects when taken by human beings. (The additional requirement of demonstrating effectiveness was added only later, in amendments to the Food and Drug Act in 1964.)

As soon as Merrell filed the application, Merrell executives began to pressure the FDA. They were anxious to have the drug on the market in time to trumpet its prospects at an upcoming convention of the American Medical Association. In many letters and phone calls and during personal trips to Washington, they sought to convey their enthusiasm for MER/29's wonderful properties. Indeed, all the test results they submitted to the FDA were exclusively favorable.

Even before approval of the application, Merrell executives were preoccupied with promotional schemes. "Let's Start Selling" was the subject of a memorandum from the company president Frank N. Getman to his chief of sales on July 27, 1959. "This is the year when we have every reason to believe Merrell should break into the truly 'big time,' " he said, offering a few of his own ideas for pushing the new drug:

> Let's take a close, critical look at the way we are stimulating the field force on MER/29. Very frankly, I have seen almost nothing going out of here in the way of good sales promotion ideas. The last revision of the detail was not very outstanding in my regard. It still seems pretty complicated for the GP, with a lot of long terms where shorter words would work. This is one that we discussed, and I find that no change was made in the closing which asked [doctors] to put 10 patients on it. Why 10? To me it makes sense to ask a doctor to try a drug on two, three or possibly five

patients, but if we're going above that, why not ask for all of them?

Why not, indeed? At first the only dissent about the value of MER/29 seemed to come from scientists at the National Heart Institute, who pointed out that while suppressing cholesterol, MER/29 might encourage the formation of desmosterol, another fatty substance whose effect was unknown. But this was merely a minor demurral, easily obscured under all the enthusiasm, and by December of that year the buildup for MER/29 had reached an even higher pitch. Merrell itself sponsored a two-day pep rally for the drug in Princeton, New Jersey, inviting almost forty scientists and doctors and paying them consultation fees in addition to full expenses. The entire conference was devoted to celebrating the drug's presumed ability to help prevent heart disease. A Cornell University medical professor summed it up with a hopeful assessment: "If more drugs had been subjected to this kind of review early in their life histories, many mistakes and millions of dollars would have been spared physicians, patients and pharmaceutical companies." Getman, on his part, later memorialized the Princeton conference as "the most terrific selling tool" Merrell had ever had.

But soon there were disquieting developments. First, the FDA asked Merrell to submit additional test data. And when Merrell did so, in February 1960, one of the FDA's pharmacologists, Dr. Edwin I. Goldenthal, examined the data and found "little margin of safety with the drug." Citing "inherent toxic potential," he urged that the FDA withhold approval of the application until clinical studies could be conducted on people taking the drug over a long period of time—several years rather than a few weeks. Other experts were also beginning to suggest that the drug might prove to be dangerous. But Merrell stood firm and, for reasons that were never entirely clear, Dr. Frank J. Talbot, a medical officer in FDA's new drug branch, decided to approve the marketing of MER/29. On April 19, 1960, he wrote Merrell that "our action in allowing this application to become effective is based solely on the evidence of the safety of the drug. All claims are on your own responsibility." In the meantime, he directed that other tests continue on people using MER/29. Within another month, Merrell submitted the required package labels to the FDA, bearing an indication under the heading "side effects" that "isolated reports have been received of nausea, vomiting, temporary vaginal bleeding and dermatitis." The assault on the potential multimillion-dollar market for an anticholesterol drug got under way officially June 1, and during the rest of 1960 an estimated 100,000 people used MER/29.

Once the drug went on sale, more reports began reaching various company officials of troubling side effects— occasional disruption of the reproductive systems in both men and women, loss of hair or a change in its color or texture, and a variety of effects on patients' eyes, including the development of cataracts. Merrell officials, among them Dr. Robert H. McMaster, then Merrell's associate director of clinical research and the mild-mannered professorial type who was sent on promotional tours of medical conventions, dismissed these incidents as flukes. Just as the new drug application was being approved, McMaster had responded to a doctor in Omaha who had complained that his patients on MER/29 suffered from eye discharge and swelling: "Most of the side effects you have reported have been unusual ones in that they have not been reported by other investigators. . . . Is it possible that [they] could have been coincidental with the administration of drugs other than MER/29 concurrently?" This same line of rebuttal was now recommended to Merrell's enthusiastic drug salesmen as well. One memorandum issued to them advised: "When a doctor says your drug causes a side effect, the immediate reply is: 'Doctor, what other drug is the patient taking?' Even if you know your drug can cause the side effect mentioned, chances are equally good the same side effect is being caused by a second drug! You let your drug take the blame when you counter with a defensive answer."

On the very day that Dr. Talbot of the FDA issued his approval of MER/29, McMaster learned of a California doctor whose results with MER/29 were "rather equivocal if not completely negative." The Californian was not ready to give up, however, and sought Merrell's financial support for an extension of his studies to other patients. "Although it begins to appear that any report from this study may be a negative one," McMaster wrote to a colleague at Merrell, "we may find that we are money ahead to keep Dr. Engelberg busy at it for a while longer rather than to take a chance on his reporting negatively on so few patients. . . . My personal recommendation is that the [$500] grant-in-aid be approved only to keep Dr. Engelberg occupied for a while longer."

Not only did Merrell seek to head off unfavorable comment on MER/29 with such tactics, but it also planted outside praise for the drug. In June 1960, McMaster drafted a laudatory letter for a physician at Hahnemann Hospital in Philadelphia, Dr. Philip Lisan, to submit to a medical journal. His experience and that of others, the letter said, indicated that "clinical side effects (nausea and skin reaction) have been almost negligible and certainly not serious." After the letter from Dr. Lisan appeared in *Medical World News,* Merrell passed a clipping along to the FDA as an example of the drug's acceptance. The management also distributed it to salesmen as an extra item for their portfolios, under the title "Dr. Lisan Speaks Up."

More criticism of MER/29 cropped up when another major drug manufacturer, Merck, conducted tests comparing the Merrell version of triparanol with its own anti-cholesterol drug that had never been marketed. In January 1961, Merck reported to Merrell that its test animals, including dogs, had developed cataracts and that several rats on the drug had gone blind. Merrell replied with shocked surprise, claiming that such symptoms had never shown up in its own tests and promising to "rerun" the Merck study itself. Merrell was later to retort that Merck's results were questionable since the competitor had used an allegedly impure supply of MER/29 for its experiments.

While proceeding with research—in effect, a delaying tactic—Merrell never bothered to notify either the FDA or the doctors to whom it supplied MER/29 samples of the negative reports. And the flow of sincere, surprised correspondence continued to issue from Cincinnati: A Pennsylvania doctor who complained of hair loss by patients was told that such cases were considered "specific drug idiosyncrasies occurring in an insignificant incidence."

Dr. John B. Chewning, a Merrell public relations man, wrote to a physician in Tomah, Wisconsin, to say that the doctor's observation of blurred vision after MER/29 therapy was "unusual"; in fact, said the reply, "we know of a paper soon to be published showing some improvement in vision in patients with diabetes and hypercholesterolomia." When doctors at the Mayo Clinic in Minnesota asked for the necessary forms to report to Cincinnati about side effects, McMaster sent along only two; the doctors at Mayo wrote back asking for at least three more. "You have underestimated us," they told McMaster jokingly.

By March of 1961, McMaster—although still writing otherwise to doctors who complained—concluded privately that "there can be no doubt of the association of MER/29 therapy with [hair] changes." He drafted a proposed addition to the warning on the drug package, citing "changes in color, texture or amount" of hair as possible side effects. That wording was vetoed on its way through the corporate power structure, however, as "rather frightening."

"After all," objected Dr. Robert T. Stormont, who vetoed the language, "none of those cases developed green, pink or lavender hair, I hope."

The warning was edited to say simply "thinning of the hair." A memo from Dr. Robert H. Woodward to H. Smith Richardson, Jr., board chairman of the parent corporation, in March 1961, confessed that the package warning had not been revised sooner "basically because we were afraid to 'stir the pot' in Washington. We have heard from several sources that FDA at times has considered reopening our . . . file but, frankly, we do not know whether this is true. The risk we run in admitting this additional side effect must be realized, however, and weighed against our moral and legal obligations." Woodward's real justification, however, seemed to come in his suggestion that the additional warning was necessary "to protect ourselves against possible damage suits."

Chairman Richardson accepted the need to revise the package warning, for his own reasons. As he wrote on his own copy of Woodward's memorandum, "Summary—can expect publications [in medical journals] on hair thinning. Important to get brochure change before this happens. Also desirable to play ball with Talbot [the FDA doctor who originally approved the new drug application] to get number 29 through over protest. Talbot has authority to O.K."

At about the same time, the name of the man who supervised Merrell's salesmen in the field began to be deleted from the list of people receiving interoffice correspondence alluding to the possible harmful consequences of MER/29. The Merrell official who left the name off said he did so because the information "might be a little discouraging" to the sales supervisor.

Merrell had a harder time coping with the issue of MER/29's effects on eyes than it did with that of the hair changes. For one thing, Dr. Talbot left the FDA in September 1961. And the man who took over his responsibility for MER/29, Dr. John O. Nestor, proved to be a somewhat more formidable administrator. When the company proposed to send to all doctors then prescribing the drug a letter that completely omitted mention of the effects on eyes, Nestor rejected it as vague and misleading. In fact, he demanded that all available eye data be brought to a meeting in Washington where MER/29 would be discussed.

That meeting took place in October 1961, but even after

it, Merrell's representatives continued to omit mention of the Merck study and other unfavorable ones during their discussions with the FDA, including one study reporting the development of cataracts in seven new test dogs in Merrell's Cincinnati laboratories. President Getman of Merrell in Cincinnati, in confidential correspondence with W. Robert Marschalk, president of the parent corporation in New York, discussed company fears that the entire existing supply of MER/29 might be seized if the firm did not cooperate adequately with the FDA; but still Merrell held out in negotiations with Nestor.

For his own part, Nestor of the FDA was now citing alarming reports about the rapid formation of desmosterol when cholesterol was cut down. In his written summary of the October meeting in Washington with Merrell officials, Nestor listed eight separate categories of disturbing side effects, including "loss of libido" and "reduced spermatogenesis," maladies that the drug company had never focused on at all. Nestor wanted the approval for MER/29 revoked, but he had trouble with his FDA superiors.

Finally, on December 1, 1961, after a running debate with Nestor that had lasted five weeks, Merrell agreed to a forthright letter of warning telling doctors about all the potential side effects of MER/29, as demanded by the FDA. But Merrell still had a two-million-dollar inventory of the miracle drug, so in two weeks the warning letter was followed by another from the company's marketing vice-president to the nation's pharmacists: "Physicians throughout the country are prescribing MER/29," it said, "and we urge you to make sure that your stocks of this high-volume specialty are adequate."

The December 1 warning letter was clearly the beginning of the end for MER/29. In early 1962, FDA statisticians were able to infer even from Merrell's own truncated data that people on the drug were three times as likely as those not taking it to develop cataracts in their eyes, and Merrell's early data were proving to have been extraordinarily optimistic. But the revelations about MER/29's development were only about to begin.

One morning in February 1962, Carson Jordan and Thomas M. Rice rode to work together in a Cincinnati car pool, as was their custom. Jordan, who worked for the telephone company, had been interested to read in the local newspapers that the Merrell company had recently been required to send out a warning letter about its anti-cholesterol drug. Jordan casually mentioned to Rice that his wife had some bad experiences while employed by the drug firm in its testing laboratories.

Rice, a regional supervisory inspector for the FDA, was intrigued. From his early days as a "food-and-drugger" in the Far Northwest, when he exposed a macaroni manufacturer for allowing rat pellets to get into his batter, Rice had relished a challenging situation and a good exposé.

At first, Rice had a hard time getting Beulah Jordan to give him information. "People contacted her and tried to keep her from talking," he now recalls. "We finally convinced her that as a public-spirited citizen she had a duty to tell us. Little by little, she would confirm things."

Mrs. Jordan's story, corroborated by others who worked at Merrell at the same time, was of a tense laboratory run by "Dr." William King, a heavy-set, gregarious type whose doctoral degree turned out to be nonexistent. King was in turn responsible to Dr. Evert Van Maanen, a quiet, scholarly man who spoke with a slight North European accent. These two supervised the collection of the test data to be used on Merrell's new drug application for MER/29.

Mrs. Jordan spoke mostly of the tests on monkeys, the most important of the tests because monkeys are closest to man on the evolutionary ladder. One day in May 1959, she said, she had made up final graphs on the monkeys only to have them rejected. Twice she was called into Van Maanen's office and asked to alter the graphs. "I raised questions concerning these changes to Mr. King," she later said, "and he told me . . . that this was what Dr. Van Maanen wanted and that I was to make the changes and keep my mouth shut. I was very disturbed and refused to initial the graph." The changes included extending the figures for the weights of eight monkeys (four normal control animals and four which were forced to take MER/ 29 in powder form) for two months beyond the period of the actual experiment, so as to create the impression that they had done well on the drug.

There was also the case of Mrs. Jordan's "pet" laboratory animal, a certain monkey. She paid special attention to that one and found that after taking MER/29 for a few months, it was unable to jump onto the weighing pan, a simple trick all the monkeys had been trained to perform. The monkey, Mrs. Jordan said, "got very mean, there was a loss of weight, and it couldn't see well enough to hit the pan. Her coat began to look scrubby . . . in our opinion, this monkey was sick due to a reaction from this drug." But one would never have known that the monkey was sick from looking at Merrell's official charts and graphs.

Although it disappeared from the laboratory without ever being sacrificed and autopsied, according to Mrs. Jordan, the monkey showed up in the new drug application submitted to FDA. In that document it was depicted as having survived normally and never having lost much weight at all. In fact, to read the charts, one would have gathered that the monkey had prospered under a heavy dosage of MER/29.

Once Rice had conducted preliminary interviews, he flew to Washington for strategy sessions on how to handle the Merrell investigation. With characteristic caution, the FDA waited six weeks—after Rice had reported the carpool conversation—before sending a team of investigators to Cincinnati. The team, when it did come, included Dr. Goldenthal, the pharmacologist who had originally been skeptical of MER/29 and had recommended against approving it without several years of additional tests. The officials at Merrell were as courteous as men of their standing are expected to be, but they were utterly unable to explain the discrepancies between laboratory books completed by Mrs. Jordan and her coworkers, on the one hand, and what had been reported to the FDA in the original application, on the other. Some of the test monkeys, it turned out, had been on MER/29 for only eight months, although they were listed in the submissions to Washington as having taken the drug for a full course of sixteen months and done well.

Subsequent investigation revealed that other employees besides Mrs. Jordan had also been directed to revise charts which did not indicate the desired results—to "smooth out data," as this revision process was called at Merrell. It was also discovered that the company had given false information to the FDA about MER/29 studies on rats. Merrell had stated that all the female rats involved in a particular experiment had survived, whereas in fact they had all died. The data submitted on their weight and blood values had been totally fabricated in the same toxicology-pathology laboratory run by King and Van Maanen. Other detrimental information about MER/29 had been withheld from the regulatory agency and from doctors— evidence of changes in monkeys' ovaries and the first reports of eye trouble in human patients, for example—although the details were fully available to each level of the corporate structure. Most of the false information submitted to the FDA had been included in brochures the company sent to doctors and had been vigorously disseminated at the 1959 Princeton conference promoting MER/29.

All permission to market MER/29 was immediately withdrawn after the FDA's two-day, on-the-scene investigation in April 1962—although the company managed to get in two extra days' worth of prescription sales while negotiating with the FDA over the exact wording of the letter withdrawing the drug. In addition to all the evidence of harmful side effects, investigators noted that there had never been substantial evidence that MER/29 actually reduced the cholesterol levels of patients, or indeed that cholesterol levels and heart disease were conclusively linked. A deputy commissioner of the FDA conceded in the spring of 1962 that "in retrospect, it is apparent that the drug should not have gone on the market in the first place."

There was, however, no official inquiry as to how the "wonder drug" had managed to obtain the agency's approval when so many people were skeptical, or why one man, Dr. Talbot, had had sole power to decide. Nor was any effort made to isolate the people in such positions from future outside pressure. (In the celebrated case of thalidomide, another Merrell product, FDA medical officer Frances O. Kelsey had stood almost alone in resisting Merrell's razzle-dazzle.)

The FDA's investigative report from Cincinnati indicated that "we feel that sufficient evidence has been obtained to support prosecution of the corporation and the individuals involved." It took time. But more than a year and a half later, with MER/29 long since off the market, a Federal grand jury in Washington returned a twelve-count indictment against the William S. Merrell Co. and its corporate parent, Richardson-Merrell Inc. Also indicted were lab supervisors Evart Van Maanen, William King, and their immediate superior, Merrell vice-president Harold Werner. The indictment cited them for lying to the FDA about rat, monkey and dog studies of MER/29, and it also accused them of fraud in their response to the observations of a Florida researcher in 1960 who claimed that MER/29 was causing cataracts to develop in the eyes of rats. The grand jury also charged that Merrell had misled the FDA and the public about the potential effects of MER/29 on conception and the dangers of taking the drug during pregnancy. The indictment, in effect, challenged virtually every statement that had ever been made on behalf of the drug.

Criminal charges against a prestigious company ranking in the *Fortune* 500 are unusual, and it was only fitting that the case against Merrell be resolved with a minimum of scandal:

With the Justice Department consenting, the Merrell

company pleaded no contest to six counts, and the senior corporation to two. All three scientists also took that recourse. In the words of Matthew F. McGuire, then chief judge of U. S. District Court for the District of Columbia, the pleas were "tantamount to a plea of guilty." But the companies had spared no expense in hiring attorneys, and they got clever ones. Chief counsel for the defendants was Lawrence Walsh, a former Federal judge and Deputy Attorney General.[1] Walsh knew there were advantages to a plea of no contest; it meant there would be no trial and thus no trial record. Merrell had worried gravely that a trial record could later be used to advantage in civil suits by people who claimed to have been injured by MER/29.

The defendants were sentenced in June 1964. Lawyer Walsh told the court on their behalf that "there certainly was no intention by this company or any of its employees to put on the market a dangerous drug. Whatever errors of judgment there were, this was not the intent. . . . Whatever these individuals did, they did what they thought they were doing on behalf of the company and, if there must be punishment, we ask that it fall on the company and not on them."

Judge McGuire could not but agree. "That is the view I have taken," he said as he levied the maximum fines of $60,000 on Merrell and $20,000 on the parent firm. "Responsibility in the background of this case," the Judge observed, "is a failure, for want of a better term, of proper executive, managerial and supervisional control . . . the

[1] Later Walsh would represent President Nixon briefly at the Paris talks on the war in Vietnam and would chair the American Bar Association committee which rubber-stamped Nixon's nominations of Haynsworth and Carswell to the Supreme Court.

responsibility of what happened falls on the company and its executive management." Instead of the five years in prison and $10,000 fine that each defendant could have received, Werner, Van Maanen and King were each sentenced merely to six months on probation.

It had, for the most part, been worth it. Richardson-Merrell was doing well, and the fines barely made a dent in the $180-million sales in fiscal 1964. The sales would have been bigger, of course, were it not for the hard luck with MER/29. But as President Marschalk told an annual meeting of stockholders (about a dozen attended) in Wilmington, Delaware, in October 1962, "There will always be some risk involved. . . . You cannot entirely remove the hazard inherent in discovering and testing and marketing new drugs." Furthermore, Judge McGuire had helped set a precedent that would be followed in his court and elsewhere on the Federal bench for years to come: If the crime is not one of obvious violence and the defendants are white gentlemen of pleasant demeanor and apparent good will, their punishment shall be mild.

That was not the end of the saga of MER/29. There has been no end yet. Even without the help of a criminal trial record, civil damage suits began to flood state and Federal courts. Many of the suits benefited from the research assistance of the "MER/29 Group," an association that eventually included almost 300 lawyers with clients who claimed to have been affected by the drug. The suits also drew upon affidavits from Mrs. Jordan and a growing body of other material implicating Merrell. Over 95 percent of the cases were settled out of court, with the drug company paying anywhere from $25,000 to $125,000, the amount varying with the seriousness of symptoms and the prevailing attitudes in the places where the complaints were brought. Several major cases did come to trial, a few of them resulting in rather spectacular jury awards of compensatory and punitive damages. In the case of Elizabeth Ostopowitz of White Plains, New York—who, after taking MER/29, suffered cataracts that required two operations for removal, was bald for several months, had her eyebrows and eyelashes turn white, and experienced painful dryness of the skin—the award ran to a total of $1.2 million (later reduced substantially by the trial judge). As one of the jurors in that trial explained the verdict, "Any criminal is certainly punished for his crimes, and this we felt was a crime so far as the company was concerned."

That view was not universally held, however. The intrinsic difficulty of regarding respectable American businesses as criminals responsible for their conduct was perhaps best reflected in a lengthy opinion by Judge Henry J. Friendly of the Second U. S. Circuit Court of Appeals, overturning the award of $100,000 in punitive damages to Sidney Roginsky, who had also taken MER/29. The problem with punitive damages, Judge Friendly wrote, was that they might be awarded repeatedly by various courts, thus subjecting Merrell to an extraordinary financial strain. Under those circumstances, "a sufficiently egregious error as to one product can end the business life of a concern that has wrought much good in the past and might otherwise have continued to do so in the future, with many innocent stockholders suffering extinction of their investments for a single management sin." What then, he mused, of the unwillingness of insurance companies to extend protection to such humanitarian enterprises which have merely stumbled briefly off the straight and narrow path?

The corporate executives were, after all, men of good intentions, Friendly seemed to say. What could be better proof of that than the fact that Werner and Van Maanen, as well as company president Getman, used MER/29 themselves right up until the moment it was withdrawn from the market? "Moreover, and this goes to a good deal of the case," the Judge wrote, "some weight must be given to the human tendency to follow a course of conduct once decided upon even when considerations have appeared that would have led to a different decision at the outset, a tendency peculiarly strong when large investments of both effort and money have been made; the very fact of the initial decision importantly affects subsequent ones." Whereupon, the Judge cited a psychology textbook. "Although this tendency can be pushed to the point of recklessness," he continued, "a court should be careful not to set the scale too low when a discovery of social utility is under review. A strong case of recklessness could have been mounted against Columbus had he returned to Palos with lives lost and nothing found."

Roginsky's lawyers, members of the "MER/29 Group," had "unearthed countless instances of carelessness and even of wilfulness by subordinate officials and of failures to exercise proper supervision and possible bad judgment by higher ones," Judge Friendly wrote. "Granted that few human endeavors would escape without blemish from such searching scrutiny, the picture is not a pretty one. But there was no proof from which a jury could properly conclude that defendant's officers manifested deliberate disregard for human welfare; what it shows as to this, apart from negligence in policing subordinates and a somewhat stiff-necked attitude toward the FDA, is rather that they were so convinced of the value of the drug both to the public welfare and to the company's finances that they maintained a sanguine view longer than prudence warranted."

A lack of prudence, in the end, was all that the appellate judge could cite against the developers and promoters of a drug that probably did far more harm than good in its life. For that lack, they have suffered little. Dr. Werner retired comfortably to a farm outside of Cincinnati. Dr. Van Maanen is teaching in the department of pharmacology at the University of Cincinnati. Dr. McMaster, who acknowledges in a smooth voice well-honed at medical conventions that there were a few "legal complications" surrounding that anticholesterol drug he once wrote so many happy letters about, is still working enthusiastically for Merrell. As for Merrell itself, it continues to prosper as part of the parent company, which for fiscal year 1971 reported a profit of $32.5 million on unprecedented sales of $408 million.

How many other similar cases there may have been before MER/29 and since, it is impossible to know. But FDA inspector Rice, now stationed at FDA headquarters in Washington and responsible for the recall of drugs, says that at the time, "I didn't think [the MER/29 case] was typical but I was wrong. . . . They were totally geared to the dollar sign. I'm sure there are many other firms similar to them—even today. I suspect [Merrell] got away with the same thing many times before. This is typical Americana: get away with what you can. I really don't think it hurt their consciences at all."

Every day American pharmaceutical firms send out announcements of new miracle drugs, new promises of paradise through medical research. They spend millions of dollars imploring doctors, institutions and clinics to try new items on their patients and then report the results. When it is convenient to do so, the drug companies themselves prepare letters and articles praising the drugs, which the doctors only have to sign and submit. Surely, many of the drugs involved are useful. But who is to calculate the cost in suffering from untold side effects, who is to count the victims of the harmful drugs, the substances introduced into human bodies by men for whom profit comes first?

In May 1959, a vice-president at Merrell wrote a memo that most chillingly reveals the mentality of such entrepreneurs. Speaking of an attempt to sell MER/29 to Armed Forces hospitals, he said frankly:

"We were not thinking here so much of honest clinical work as we were of a premarketing softening prior to the introduction of the product."

CHAPTER FIVE

"This Napalm Business"

by SAUL FRIEDMAN

IT was an early morning program. It had begun with the day's violence from Vietnam, and now the television interviewer was making an effort to be as tactful as possible with his guests, the gentlemen from the Dow Chemical Company who had asked for time to reply to their critics.

Interviewer: "Whatever its other achievements—and they are considerable—Dow, in the minds of many people, means Napalm. Why would you continue as the manufacturer of a product that's causing such a headache?"

Herbert Dow Doan, then the company president: "This Napalm is a good discriminate, strategic weapon, and we feel those folks oughta have it."

Interviewer: "Is there any other use [for Napalm] besides destroying life by fire?"

Carl Gerstacker, Dow chairman: "At the present time, we don't know of any other use. It has been suggested that it be used to burn up waste."

Twenty-five years before, when it was first developed, that had been one of the smaller scientific problems with Napalm: It had virtually no use apart from delivering one of the more horrible means of death. Chemist Louis F. Fieser of Harvard University's Gibbs Laboratory noted that shortcoming in the paper that disclosed his wartime discovery of Napalm.

"According to an officer who inspected some of the Japanese areas devastated by the B-29 raids with M-69 [fire] bombs," Fieser wrote, "a few of the more enterprising civilians salvaged a dud or two and made good use of the recovered Napalm for cooking and heating. Certain other uses of a more novel and scientific character are being investigated with promising results. [But] it is too early as yet to know whether Napalm will find significant application in times of peace."

Nevertheless, Fieser and his team of five Harvard colleagues (who went on to jobs in the drug, chemical, and explosives industries) barely concealed their pride when they reported on the discovery of Napalm and uses "of which we had not even dreamed." In flame-throwers Napalm was "spectacular," they said. And bellytank fire bombs "proved effective in driving the enemy out of caves and underground defensive installations, and in burning out whole areas held by stubbornly resisting Japanese troops."

Their research was done in 1941–42, but security requirements delayed publication of their paper until the August, 1946, issue of *Industrial and Engineering Chemistry,* exactly a year after Hiroshima and Nagasaki. And Army chemical-warfare experts, as if competing for a place in the sun that science, industry, and the military had created over those Japanese cities, beat the drum for the use of Napalm in future wars.

The development of Napalm actually began during the First World War with partially successful attempts to thicken gasoline. When it was used in bombs, the result was an instantaneous fireball like the kind that ancient Greeks and Persians made from crude oil, pitch and asphalt. But the fireball tended to blow itself out, and damage was confined. It was therefore ineffective compared to high explosives, the manufacture of which took higher priority over incendiaries.

If World War I was the rehearsal, the Second World War, even as it began, became the full-scale performance of total war, a struggle which engulfed whole nations, its cities, and civilians. In a war fed by ideology and waged between peoples as well as armies, incendiaries became invaluable because their plague by fire terrorized and demoralized as widely as they destroyed.

One type of incendiary, copied by the United States from the "Elektron" bombs used by the Italians in Ethiopia and the Nazis in Spain, was composed of Thermit and a combustible magnesium alloy produced here by the Dow Chemical Company. It proved to be a successful weapon, but early in the war magnesium was expensive and in short supply. The monopoly of Dow Chemical, the Government said, was one reason for the critical shortage. Indeed, a Federal grand jury, in 1941, charged that Dow, among others, had entered into a conspiracy to monopolize magnesium production, which in effect gave the Germans indirect control of the magnesium market in the years prior to American entry into the war, and limited the domestic supplies.

Dow angrily denied the charges and complained that there had been no market for magnesium in the United States before the war, and no official appreciation of its value. Therefore, Dow said, despite its best efforts to sell magnesium, it was forced to limit production. Dow went on during the war to become a large producer of magnesium. But the company chose not to contest the conspiracy charges in court; it signed an agreement to stop what it denied it had been doing, and it paid fines totaling $140,000.

Willard H. Dow, then president of the company, later explained that Dow and its officers "could not at the same time be in a court defending their honor and be in a factory defending their country. They had no choice, in April 1942, but to placate by pleading *nolo contendere* and agreeing to a consent decree. They had to submit to indignity in order to get on with the business of war."

Against the background of the magnesium shortage, the Chemical Warfare Service concluded that bombs of jellied gasoline would be much cheaper than magnesium weapons. The problem was finding a jelling agent. So before Pearl Harbor, in the summer of 1941, Fieser began work on the problem with the Chemical Corps at the Edgewood Arsenal in Maryland. Early experiments, Fieser reported, "convinced us of the potential value of a gelled hydrocarbon fuel that would be distributed over a target area in the form of burning, adherent masses."

Rubber was used in the first experiments. But the attack on Pearl Harbor and the fall to the Japanese of rubber-producing areas of Southeast Asia forced the researchers to look elsewhere for a jelling agent. A number of chemical companies (not including Dow) joined in the research effort, as well as the oil industry, the Hercules Powder Company (which hired two of Fieser's associates), Arthur D. Little Company, Inc., Armour and Company, and even the U. S. Food and Drug Administration.

In all the research literature no questions, no qualms were raised about the manufacture of Napalm or the consequences of its use in warfare. The laboratory process, the language of chemical journals, and the division of labor left no room for such questions. Besides, Germany and Japan were popular enemies, and after huge portions of London were set aflame in 1940 with magnesium incendiaries, the development of Napalm became a matter of fighting fire with fire.

After months of experiments with a number of substances, Fieser reported success on January 29, 1942, the date Napalm, a benign-looking, milky-white jelly, bubbled into being like a devil's brew.

Fieser merely recorded "that a combination of aluminum napthenate with aluminum palmitate [soaps from fatty acids and coconut oils] could easily be incorporated into gasoline to form a promising gel, and we termed this napthenate-palmitate combination a Napalm gel."

In the quiet of the Cambridge laboratory, there were no celebrations, only a laconic report on the completion of work under Contract OEMsr-179. The Army and industry took it from there, and Napalm was used for the first time in flame-throwers during December 1942, against the Japanese on Guadalcanal. Its success was unqualified.

An Army chemical-warfare expert wrote: "Unlike the Germans who usually fought well but retreated when the situation became hopeless, the Japanese soldier usually defended his foxhole, pillbox or bunker to the death regardless of the odds against him. He constructed intricate and amazingly strong positions which were very difficult to neutralize by conventional means. No weapon proved so effective against this type of target as the flame-thrower."

From the beginning, then, Napalm evaded the Geneva agreements which outlawed poison gas, which also had been designed specifically to rout the enemy from his trenches or "neutralize" him if he foolishly chose to fight on against overwhelming odds. Napalm, like mustard gas, frightens victims, poisons and suffocates them to death if they are not incinerated. However, the flame-thrower was at least selective and aimed against military installations and personnel. The Napalm fire bomb was deliberately designed as an indiscriminate terror weapon for mass destruction and death among civilians.

Colonel M. E. Barker could not contain his excitement as he wrote about fire bombs among "Future Chemical Warfare Possibilities" in the July 1947 issue of the *Chemical Corps Journal.* "Even the atomic bomb did not equal the destructiveness of a single massed incendiary air attack in either the number of persons killed or the amount of enemy property destroyed." And with an eye on future budgets, he added: "One atomic bomb was far more expensive than the whole lot of incendiaries."

The first fire-bomb raid against Japan, on March 9, 1945, he said, was aimed at "the most inflammable section of Tokyo," the poorer, residential areas where the crowded houses are made from wood and paper.

"A huge fire was started that burned out over fifteen

square miles of area and shot flames into the sky so high that they could be seen two hundred miles away. The results were so astounding that all the incendiary bombs available were dropped in the week, and it was a month before the supply could be replenished and incendiary bombing resumed."

Napalm had been used briefly in the European Theater, against the German fortresses on the French Coast. And there were devastating magnesium incendiary attacks against Dresden and Hamburg. But the terror of sticky fire was reserved mostly for the cities of Japan, and Japanese troops (as well as natives) on the Pacific Islands. (On Saipan, Napalm attacks razed the island and panicked thousands of Japanese and Saipanese into suicide.)

In the October, 1947, *Chemical Corps Journal,* L. Wilson Greene, the scientific director of the Army's Chemical Center, wrote that fire bombs alone had destroyed more than one hundred sixty square miles of the principal Japanese cities. "In Europe," he wrote, "only 6 percent of the total bombing tonnage dropped was made up of incendiaries, while in Japan the ratio was approximately 20 percent of the total. If the war had been prolonged, it was planned to drop on Japan a tonnage of incendiary bombs equal to that of high-explosive bombs." As if campaigning for the future of the Chemical Warfare Corps, Barker said incendiaries had already sealed the doom of Japan when the atomic bombs were dropped. Hiroshima and Nagasaki, he said, merely served as "a perfect face-saver, so important in oriental politics."

Barker lovingly described the simplicity of the fire bomb: "the American tin can filled with jellied gasoline." But it was not good enough, he said. "What we need and will get is a filling at least twice as dense and more sticky than gasoline which will burn more fiercely and will have a higher heat content per unit of volume than does gasoline," he wrote. Future incendiary bombs, he predicted, would be three times as effective as those used in the Second World War. And he added: "We will get it if we have to jell mustard gas and use this as an incendiary filling."

Mustard gas in any form had been outlawed at Geneva. But it is instructive to note that our military chemists were thinking along these lines in the peacetime year of 1947.

It is no comfort to the dead and disfigured of Indochina that it did not become necessary to turn to mustard gas. In the mid-sixties, the United States, with a certain childlike delight over a new toy called "flexible response" and a Teutonic preoccupation with even the grizzliest technology, began the development of an exquisitely novel array of weapons for counterinsurgency. One of them, produced by chemists at Eglin Air Force Base in Florida, was a new, improved brand of Napalm.

Napalm-B it was called. And instead of soap, a plastic called polystyrene was used as the jelling agent. It produced just the right balance for killing—thin enough to spread over great distances, thick enough to adhere to anything it touched. With a mixture of two parts polystyrene and one part each of gasoline and benzene, a six-pound bomb could splatter an area the size of a football field with sticky flame as hot as 2000 degrees, capable of burning up to twenty minutes. And as if the makers had decided to twist the knife, magnesium or phosphorous—bits of which, still burning, could penetrate the flesh—was added to the mixture, the better to ignite it.

The ingredient that made it all work was the polystyrene. And the Air Force turned to the largest American supplier of the plastic—the Dow Chemical Company. The company which had contributed to the shortage of magnesium twenty-five years before, and indirectly to the development of jellied gasoline as a substitute, thus became the country's largest producer of Napalm-B.

In early 1966, the first Napalm-B contracts were awarded to Dow and to a United Aircraft subsidiary, the United Technology Center, which purchased its polystyrene supplies from Dow. Throughout World War II, 97,000 tons of fire bombs—194 million pounds—were dropped on Japan. The amount of Napalm-B ordered by the Air Force from Dow and United in the initial, one-year contracts totaled 150 million pounds.

United got out of the Napalm business after a year and left it entirely to Dow. And eventually Napalm production at Dow's plant in Torrance, California, where the ingredients were mixed and the canisters filled, increased to as much as 50 million pounds a month. Yet Herbert (Ted) Doan, who served as Dow president from 1962 to 1971, says he knew nothing of the Napalm contracts until late in 1966 when the peace movement began its campaign against the company.

"We were in this before we knew it," said Doan in an interview. "You don't run around and approve every order that any salesman makes or anything that's going on with the Government. Our government affairs people went out and got this order because we make polystyrene, and it wasn't until the public furor came along that this thing got examined."

His ignorance may seem difficult to believe, since the Air Force, with industry cooperation, shrouded the Napalm-B procurement program in secrecy for fear of anti-war demonstrators. It seems reasonable to assume that the companies, engaged in trying to protect themselves from public reaction, had to have known what was going on. Furthermore, the entire United States production of polystyrene was about 60 million pounds a month in 1965, before the Napalm-B orders were placed. Trade journals predicted the Air Force would use another 25 million pounds a month, a projected increase which could not have gone unnoticed at Dow. Apparently it didn't, for shortly before large-scale military buying began, Dow raised the price of polystyrene from nine to ten cents a pound.

Still, it is possible that neither Doan nor Dow chairman Carl Gerstacker personally knew what their company was getting into. The $6.5-million Napalm contract represented only a fraction of Dow's sales (then at $1.3 billion, now nearly $2 billion). Dow produces more than one thousand products for industrial and home use, ranging from caustic soda to Saran Wrap. And the Torrance plant, where fewer than a dozen men worked, is only one of seventy-four in twenty states and seventeen countries which employ forty-seven thousand people.

Furthermore, in 1962 Dow had switched to team leadership, which was more efficient and specialized than the old hierarchical system but more impersonal and divided in responsibility. It was impossible and unnecessary under such a structure for a single executive to examine every contract. And when the government affairs office in Washington gladly complied with an Air Force request to supply polystyrene for Napalm, it was normal to notify only the divisions involved in fulfilling the contract.

Dow is basically a company founded on research and

science, but little science was necessary to begin Napalm production. Even if the skill of the laboratory had been needed, however, the industrial scientist at Dow had become so far removed from the final product it is doubtful he would have alerted management to the implications of manufacturing Napalm. Dr. Turner Alfrey, Jr., a senior Dow chemist in the field of polymers, said: "When we complete a process, it is taken from us by the production people, the finance people, the marketing people, and the sales people. We have nothing more to do with it."

Since the thirties, Dow has spent more time than most companies examining products for possible harmful effects before they are marketed. Dow, for example, has been a pioneer in studying possible genetic effects. Yet Dow's scientists did not consider the damage hundreds of pounds of Dow mercury waste were doing to fish and, indirectly, to human beings. And rather than employ wide margins of safety, which may prevent the marketing of a new product, Dow scientists were often obliged to work with margins—as in the production of plutonium and defoliants—which outside experts denounced as too close.

Nor did the corporate structure, as it grew more specialized, allow the scientists or the executive to wonder about the possible consequences of their acts. There is strong pressure on the scientist to create to sell. And intellectually his profession and his laboratory are more confining than the executive suite. Even Doan despairs at the narrow parochialism of his scientists.

Besides, despite occasional spats, the modern corporation deems itself to be, and is in fact, an extension of the state in its style and in its loyalty to long-range national policy. In 1956, almost as if it were propounding a message on the state of the union, Dow's management announced that as part of American Industry it had helped build the national capacity for guns and butter.

Like other corporations with far-flung interests, Dow could not exist without the protection of the United States Government. Dow's interests and the Government's, therefore, tend to coincide. Dow executives, so conventional in their views, do not challenge basic Government policies, especially those that generate need for Dow's products, unless by fluke they are clearly against the company's interests. Where there is no challenge, there is no questioning and no meaningful decision to be made at the top. Ted Doan, in an interview, said he had rejected only once a request from the Government to engage in defense work—the research and development of chemical and biological weapons. Doan had not attempted to relate such research to the national interest. He merely had not wished to risk Dow's position in the marketplace. "Frankly, in today's environment," Doan said, "if they want that kind of work done, they should do it in-house, and you people who don't like it can go at the Government and they can take the social brunt of it. It's just plain not worth it for an industrial concern to do it."

But when public attention forced Dow to answer for its manufacture of Napalm, Doan's stock reply was that it was doing so only in the national interest.

Dow was founded at the turn of the century by Ted Doan's grandfather, Herbert H. Dow, upon a new process for extracting bromines and other chemicals from brine. For most of its history it has been a closely knit company, and in refusing to move its corporate headquarters from Midland, Michigan, where it began, it has tried to hang on to its provincial origins, its sense of family and community.

However, under the leadership of Dow's son-in-law, Leeland A. Doan, Ted's father, Dow went international (although, as shown, it had had international relations before then). And the younger Doan, who was only forty when he became president in 1962, reorganized the executive structure of the company so that it would be more responsive to the computerized, technological outlook of the times.

An intense and wiry man with a folksy, nasal, midwestern twang, Doan talks from whichever side of his mouth is not occupied by a large cigar. He looks younger than his forty-eight years and has that shirt-sleeve approach which puts visitors, and the college youngsters with whom he likes to speak, at ease. He prides himself on his avocation, which is philosophy, the Durants being among his favorites.

Doan was born in Midland, and he always knew that no matter where he went he would come back there—to the company. He attended public schools in Midland, and Cranbrook, a private school near Detroit, before going to Cornell. After an interruption of two years in the Air Corps and his marriage to a Michigan girl, Doan returned to Cornell, won a degree—in chemical engineering, naturally —and in 1949 began his years at Dow. His father sent him through the company training course and put him to work in various departments before nominating him for the board in 1953. Like his father, Ted Doan sought new Dow products for new markets, such as home and agricultural use, and acquisitions and plants abroad. He was named executive vice-president in 1960, and two years later, on the retirement of his father, Ted Doan was elected president.

The Dow family holds 12.5 percent of the company stock, but exercises considerable influence over much more. So Doan had, within the limits of corporate politics, a free hand as he brought a kind of youth revolution to the company management. Tough and messianic, Doan set out to reduce the power of division managers who, as friends and cronies from the old days, had built empires within the company. Doan's ideal was group decision-making and teamwork. And at Dow's top, he built a tri-umvirate with himself in charge of planning, Carl Ger-stacker in charge of finance, and C. B. (Ben) Branch as executive vice-president in charge of operations.

Gerstacker said of the reorganization: "We operate largely on the basis of group decisions and with a sur-prising amount of overlapping of duties and responsibili-ties. We are in many respects the opposite of a military organization with its carefully defined lines and bounds of authority."

And Branch said: "Where top management act as long-range leaders of change, middle management will increas-ingly act as managers of change. They will have new, broader charters to run day-to-day operations. In fact, they will take over many of top management's jobs of today, leaving the top men free to carry out broader responsi-bility."

It is questionable, in the corporate structure, whether such a concept means more independent values and de-cision-making below or an abdication of responsibilities on top. In any event, the reorganization created a new government affairs department in Washington, which lob-

bied for the company's interests and aggressively sought
Federal contracts.

It was just after Dow had passed the billion-dollar mark
in sales and had stepped tentatively into the home-products
market that its manufacture of Napalm-B produced a back-
splash, so to speak. The first, relatively unpublicized,
demonstrations against Dow were held on May 28, 1966,
at Torrance and at the company offices in New York's
Rockefeller Center, just two months after work on the
Napalm contract began.

For the first time Dow's top executives, most of whom
sat on the board, discussed the company's involvement
with Napalm. Dow, its public relations men suggested,
was at a disadvantage. Unlike some other companies which
produced more weapons than did Dow, it was not really
a home-products company with a built-in favorable image
among consumers and a diverting television slogan. Its
customers were industrial users.

With a year to go on the contract and the antiwar
movement still confined to a small band of radicals, Dow
decided to continue the manufacture of Napalm and to
present a low profile to the protesters. Dow public relations
chief Ellis N. Brandt said the tactic was designed to "minimize damage."

Dow issued a statement which said, in part: "Our position on the manufacture of Napalm is that we are a supplier
of goods to the Defense Department and not a policy-
maker. We do not and should not try to decide military
strategy or policy. Simple good citizenship requires that
we supply our government and our military with those
goods which they feel they need whenever we have the
technology and capability and have been chosen by the
government as the supplier."

Just as government officials miscalculated the course of the war and domestic dissent, Dow underestimated the abhorrence of Napalm itself as a weapon of the war and a rallying issue for protest. Like its Michigan neighbor General Motors, then under assault from the consumer movement, Dow saw itself singled out unfairly. It could not fathom the swiftly rising tide against the mindless machinery of corporate America, whether it helps make war or manipulates the marketplace. In August 1966, Midland, which under Dow's beneficent dominance had become a prosperous, lily-white, middle-class bastion for the right wing in Michigan, was treated to the sight of pickets from the University of Michigan chapter of Students for a Democratic Society.

In the following months, the protests against Napalm and Dow grew in number and intensity. Members of the board, which includes only a few from outside Dow, were in regular contact with each other, puzzling out "this Napalm business." Some were hard-nosed and determined to ignore the protests. But most were uncomfortable.

Doan's four children were split over the issue. Like their mother, Donalda, they had caught the contagion of the antiwar movement. And in March 1967, when Gerstacker returned from a trip to South America, he had a letter on his desk from an old friend, James H. Laird, a minister with the American Friends Service Committee. Laird had read in a National Association of Manufacturers publication of a talk Gerstacker had given to a group of clergymen, defending the manufacture of Napalm and asking for the church's opinion.

"I am not the church but I am a churchman, and perhaps my twenty-five years as a Christian minister permit me at least to express an opinion," Laird wrote to Gerstacker.

"I think Napalm is a morally outrageous weapon and its use utterly unjustifiable."

Enclosing pictures of Napalm victims, Laird added: "Imagine how we would feel if these were our children. Could we be persuaded that any political objective justified visiting such indignity on human beings?"

Gerstacker had said that Dow is in business to benefit society as a whole, and Laird asked him, "If a North Vietnamese corporation had the industrial capacity to manufacture Napalm to be dropped on us, would you say that it would be making a contribution that benefited society as a whole?"

Laird asked: "Is not society all of mankind?"

Gerstacker was troubled by Laird's letter and said so. He said that Dow's board of directors and management had been deliberating the Napalm issue with great earnestness. He noted the Pentagon's pledge that care would be taken to avoid Napalming civilians. And he recalled a tour of South Vietnam by Dr. Howard Rusk, director of the Institute of Rehabilitation Medicine at the New York University Medical Center, who reported he had not seen any Napalm-burned children.

Gerstacker nevertheless acknowledged that civilians were being burned by Napalm. And he admitted that he would be distressed if it were American children who were being burned. But no, he said, the use of Napalm by the North Vietnamese would not be justified, because they were committing aggression against the South Vietnamese and were attempting to take away their freedom.

He had felt uncomfortable, he said, when Laird suggested that governments can be wrong and that the Germans who cooperated with Hitler were wrong. But Gerstacker replied that he had attended government briefings in Washington and knew that the American Government was not similar to Hitler's. He said Laird and others who opposed Napalm weren't concentrating on the pertinent question. It was not a matter of the type of weapon, he said. He asked whether Laird would have felt better about a German industrialist who had refused to make the ovens in which Jews were to be killed because he considered them a less humane instrument than machine guns. Gerstacker wondered if the German clergymen had eased their consciences by objecting to the kind of weapons used to murder the Jews.

Gerstacker had served for a time on the Business Advisory Council to the anti-poverty program, and called on that background to make a final argument.[1] We have compelled young Americans, he said, many of whom are poor, to fight in Vietnam. Would Laird deprive them of the most effective weapons? Was it now right for America to give weapons to these underprivileged soldiers that were merely the equal of those of the enemy? Was this how Laird would provide equality for these boys? The more he thought about Laird's argument and his own rejoinders, Gerstacker said, the more he favored the manufacture of Napalm.

In the Dow organization, however, a few of the employees and scientists and some of the stockholders began voicing their feeling that the company ought to get out of the Napalm business. Doan countered by obtaining a per-

[1] He also used his position on the Advisory Council to ask then Vice-President Hubert Humphrey to intervene on behalf of Dow's attempts to have the Lake Huron port of Bay City, near Midland, declared a "foreign trade zone," which would entitle Dow to get cheaper oil feedstocks for its operations.

sonal letter from Secretary of Defense Robert McNamara complimenting Dow workers and shareowners on the service the company was performing.

Meanwhile, protests aimed at Dow recruiters spread among the most prestigious campuses—Yale, Harvard, Brandeis, Chicago, the Universities of California, Wisconsin, Minnesota, and Michigan. The company's California public relations man, Jack Jones, helped Dow very little when he told campus protesters that pictures of Napalm-burned civilians were "as phony as can be."

"There are no skin burns from Napalm," he said. "It burns right through or kills by concussion and suffocation . . . We're not involved in a football game . . . a game with rules."

Dow's board met again in late 1967 to discuss, among other things, Napalm. And after furious debate, it agreed to the forthcoming follow-on contract. But at Doan's insistence, it decided no longer to lay low against the storm. Dow's response to the protests would be to escalate its public relations effort.

Doan, a pugnacious, hard-sell salesman, led the new campaign. His replies to critics were direct but conciliatory. He suggested the dialogue, however raucous at times, was a good thing; it was making the company and the nation think. "The [Napalm] contract has little economic significance to Dow," he said repeatedly. "It amounted to less than one half of one percent of total sales—in the range of five million dollars . . . We are not a major defense contractor. All of our business to all branches of government comes to less than five percent of sales."

The argument was somewhat misleading. First, while Napalm sales were a fraction of Dow's total, they accounted for a large portion of the company's polystyrene sales. The overhead at Torrance was so small that the return on Dow's investment in the Napalm program was huge. And $5 million each year purchased quite enough Napalm to cover South Vietnam.

Secondly, a document taken from Dow's Washington office by an antiwar raiding party in 1969 entitled "U. S. Government Marketing Department—Five-year Plan—1967–1971," contains this statement:

"The [sales] figures [like those used by Doan] represent a direct sales approach . . . They do not, however, give a true indication of the total impact of the Government or the 'war' on Dow's sales. This can only be accomplished when an adequate method of reporting secondary sales [sales to companies and/or distributors who in turn sell directly to the Government] is developed. This will reveal such sales activities as Dow's share of the $20-million plastic ammunition container business, the tons of aluminum and magnesium that go into military and space programs, and the quantity of chemicals and plastics that move through distributors and fabricators into government applications. . . . All of these represent sizable dollar volume that is almost impossible to retrieve except on the basis of personal knowledge of accounts."

The memorandum also informed management that "there will be [Dow] product requirements dictated by either the continuation of the Vietnam situation or other situations that might be created because of military conflict."

In his frank exchanges with students, his articles in the *Wall Street Journal* and the house organ *Dow Diamond*, and in interviews, Doan sought to shift attention from

Napalm to the war itself. And, like Gerstacker, he pronounced himself a dove. Neither of them, however, publicly joined the opposition of the war. "We don't feel that in our position as company representatives, we can say anything we darn please," Doan said. "We don't feel that we should put pressure on the Government in areas we do not understand. We really don't know what the [Vietnam] objectives are, and the tactics and the strategies. Even as an individual I would be speaking for Dow.

"If you took a vote in Dow, it's my belief—and we have certain evidence of this—that ninety percent of the people would support us on our Napalm position. We got a lot of hardhats. What morality or knowledge or anything do I have that would give me the right to take a position on something I don't know anything about? I think we got a lot of hypocritical nonsense going on in industrial statements. The people in industry get too enthusiastic about social problems and they don't know what they're talking about.

"What they know is how to make money in an industrial concern—we hope ethically and with moral judgment. But they are not experts on foreign policy. They are not experts on the ghetto. I think it would be a dangerous thing indeed if industrial people decided to take it upon themselve to judge what the folks in the United States want."

Dow has, on numerous occasions, made judgments on legislation and policy in the national government and in the states where its plants are located. And its lobbyists, like those of most corporations, have sought in subtle and overt ways to influence policy. When Doan became president of Dow, for example, one of his Michigan congressmen, James

Harvey, tossed a reception for him to meet other law-makers. Dow's airplane has been put at the disposal of key members of Congress. Dow's Washington representatives help funnel campaign contributions to members of the House and Senate. As Gerstacker pointed out, Dow officials have been given briefings (which they always seemed to accept uncritically) not available to the general public. And Dow lobbyists have even supplied gifts of Saran Wrap to the wives of legislators.

Nevertheless, Doan's primary point is a crucial one. How can a corporation, which is a creature of government, survive if it cannot serve government when called on? And if, like Dow, it has substantial interests and business agreements (much like diplomatic alliances) in sensitive places like Greece, Portugal, Spain, Japan, Chile, Colombia, and Brazil, how can it separate its policies from its government's?

Would it not indeed be dangerous for a united corporate community to second-guess government, even for the best of reasons? The complaint today of the antiwar and consumer movements is that the Government is in league with corporations or vice versa. But these same movements are just as enraged when corporate power challenges the Government's policies on pollution controls, for example.

Despite Doan's efforts, and a stepped-up public relations campaign which suggested that while Dow was being condemned for producing Napalm it was given no credit for manufacturing a successful measles vaccine (Lirugen) and other useful drugs and chemicals, the protests increased. Dow was forced to cancel campus visits of recruiters as anti-Napalm demonstrations in 1968 hit one out of every three colleges. That fall, scientists at Midland formed the

"Dow Interdisciplinary Group," which was to meet regularly to exchange ideas and communicate with management its concerns over the direction of research and the uses to which it is put.

In early 1969, antiwar groups vandalized Dow's headquarters in Midland and its government affairs office in Washington. Dow was embarrassed when some of the documents, one of which was a list of campaign contributions of questionable legality, were turned over to the press. At the same time a small stockholder group threatened to challenge company executives at Dow's 1969 annual meeting. And in upper Michigan, when a member of the Dow family volunteered to do publicity work for a committee campaigning on behalf of a national park, he was told: "We don't need your kind of public relations."

The annual meeting, on May 7, was held in Dow's home town, Midland. And in hostile surroundings, the little bank of stockholder dissidents, led by the Medical Committee on Human Rights, were listened to and overwhelmingly rejected. In a thirty-minute rebuttal to the committee spokesman, Gerstacker said: "There's a rumor that we're going out of the Napalm business. Let me say clearly, It's not true. We are producing Napalm now. We expect to bid on other Government contracts, and if successful [we] will continue producing it." The crowd of 1200 greeted Gerstacker's words with loud and prolonged applause. But his words and the ovation had a touch of bravado. For Dow insiders knew that the Torrance plant was about to complete the current Napalm contract. And they doubted the company would get or want another one.

The company had improved the polystyrene production

process which gave Dow the capacity to turn out 750 million pounds of it a year in the United States, and nearly two billion pounds throughout the world. Dow was the world leader in polystyrene and hoped to expand its use in packaging, housewares, and toys. The manufacture of polystyrene for Napalm and the possibility of boycotts and further critical publicity threatened to put a crimp in those hopes for expansion.

Besides, the antiwar movement was becoming broad and popular in 1969. And there were other troubles looming for Dow. Protests were mounting against defoliation in Vietnam, and there were indications that chemicals like the 2,4,5-T sold to the Government by Dow (for $6.8 million annually) were causing genetic defects. In Colorado, a fire at a plant run by Dow to produce plutonium (for warheads) endangered the area with radioactivity. And there were reports that quantities of poisonous metallic mercury found in Lake Erie, Lake St. Clair and nearby tributaries between Michigan and Canada, had come from Dow's plants.

In the summer of 1969, Dow's board and management, deeply divided, struggled over whether and how to bid on the new, upcoming Napalm contract. Although some hardliners suggested the company go after the contract aggressively, most directors and executives wanted to be rid of it—but with saved face.

They were given an opening by the American Electric Co. of Los Angeles, which had been the Pentagon's prime contractor in the manufacture of the Napalm canisters. Dow had mixed and supplied the filling. Dow was now notified that American Electric intended to produce the filling itself, and would bid on the entire contract—Napalm as well as canisters. Some company sources suggest that Dow, to get off the Napalm hook, helped American Electric or promised to supply the polystyrene. Dow denies both assertions.

In any case, Dow executives decided to take a middle course between a hard-line low bid and a deliberately losing high bid. They set a price which was identical to the previous year—about twelve cents a pound—suggesting it really was a low bid because of inflation. However, the price of polystyrene had been kicked up over the years. And Dow's improved processes for polystyrene production made it possible for the company to produce it cheaper. Moreover, Dow must have known that American Electric, no longer required to subcontract the filling to Dow, could make a lower bid, which it did.

In November 1969, American Electric, as expected, took over the production of Napalm. And it has since galled Dow executives that American Electric has not become a target for large-scale protests. Indeed, Robert W. Dowling, the chairman of City Investing Co., which owns American Electric, is considered a leading liberal Democrat, and was an influential contributor to the New York gubernatorial campaign of Arthur J. Goldberg.[2]

Ted Doan maintains that Dow took the correct approach when it met the Napalm controversy head on, although members of his board disagree. But he is happy "this Napalm problem" is done with. And partly because of

---

[2] A number of companies, like City Investing, Bulova Watch, Avco, Motorola, Aluminum Company of America, Honeywell, Sperry Rand, Cessna Aircraft, Uniroyal, Westinghouse, the Brunswick Corp., General Time, and Hamilton Watch have developed and manufactured the cruelest antipersonnel weapons, like phosphorous mines and pellet bombs, without hearing any real protest.

the controversy, and because he discovered the world outside the corporation during his campus forays and wants to know more about it, Doan, on February 4, 1971, suddenly, without warning and without future plans, notified his board that at forty-eight he had had enough. Giving up a salary of $249,000 a year, he quit as president (although he remained as a director). More significant, the leadership of the company passed for the first time out of the Dow family, to Ben Branch, the executive vice-president.

About the same time, as part of the efforts to shed the skin of the Napalm image and to push Dow a bit further into consumer merchandise, the company's market men began testing two new products, even passing samples out to secretaries on Capitol Hill.

One was "Touch of Sweden," a lotion to prevent chapping. Another was "Aztec," a jellied substance to prevent sunburn.

CHAPTER SIX

Men of Distinction

by JAMES BOYD

"A *good merger is like marrying a rich woman and taking her money. It's as sweet as that, sweeter even, because you can have as many of these brides as you want and you don't have to live with them any longer than you want to. Or it's like politics. You can often get control and speak for the majority with only 10 percent of the voting stock, because you're organized while the mass of stockholders are strung out and don't pay much attention. Best of all, you do it with borrowed money. Never use your own.*

"You start out with control of a little fleabag company that's ready for the receivers. Then you find a fat corporation that's been selling its assets and is sitting on lots of cash. You send in a spy to find out where the 'control stock' is; usually it's held by directors of the company. You bribe them, in a manner of speaking, by offering to buy the company stock they hold at a price much higher than it's worth; in return, they agree to resign and appoint your men in their places. Then you go to your bank, let them in on the deal, offer their key men personal stock options and other side deals—and they'll loan you all you need to buy out the directors. Once you're in control of the new company, you use some of its assets to pay off your bank and divvy up what's left with your insiders. The only way you can do that legally, of course, is to merge your new company with the old one you've just about bankrupted. That way the new entity assumes all your old debts.

"Stockholders? They don't know anything about it, really. You've already bought out their leaders. All they see is what's on the proxy statement—and you're the fellow who puts it out, because you're the management now. Hide your old company's debts, doctor up the figures, hire one of those New York evaluating firms to back you up, and always promise the exact opposite of what you plan to do. Like I said, it's just like politics. And don't waste your time worrying about the courts or the SEC. Don't they always take the side of management? Only one thing —you have to keep mergerin' or it will catch up with you."

Confession of an Anonymous Mergerer

I

Every society proclaims a close relationship between its dominant group and Almighty God. It was inevitable therefore that in America businessmen would somehow expropriate the Lord. For many a dark Calvinist decade, success in business was held to be a sign of righteousness and of God's favor. Even when this assumption began to lose hold, corporate leaders still were invested with an aura of legitimacy, respectability and capability not accorded to politicians, academics or professional men.

Vast blunders and indescribable rogueries slowly dispelled that aura. It was all right for the public at large to be gulled by business, under the rule of *caveat emptor,* but for *stockholders* to be bamboozled by their own management, that was intolerable. A restorative was required— regulatory laws; for a business society, a nation of investors, must retain belief in the integrity of corporate processes and of the men who manage them.

And so the corporate officer or director has become ringed about with legal prohibitions. He may not buy or sell stocks on the basis of inside information not available to the investing public; may not benefit himself at the expense of his corporation; may not conceal relevant information from the stockholders on matters requiring their vote; may not misrepresent the facts to other directors or stockholders; may not leave the interests of the corporation undefended against the machinations of predators; may not borrow money to buy stocks beyond the limits of margin requirements. Behind these laws stands a vast array of prosecutors, courts and regulatory agencies.

Justice Benjamin Cardozo gave classic expression to the obligations of a corporate trustee:

> Many forms of conduct permissible in a workaday world for those acting at arm's length, are forbidden to those bound by fiduciary ties. A trustee is held to something stricter than the morals of the market place. Not honesty alone, but the punctilio of an honor the most sensitive, is then the standard of behavior. As to this there has developed a tradition that is unbending and inveterate. Uncompromising rigidity has been the attitude of courts of equity when petitioned to undermine the rule of undivided loyalty.

Or so we have been led to believe.

II

It was Friday the 13th of December, 1968, but to Herbert Korholz, president of the Susquehanna Corporation, the portents had never seemed so favorable. As he savored his morning coffee, the *Wall Street Journal* was trumpeting to all who mattered the news of his $2-billion proposal to seize control of the American Smelting and Refining Company, giant of copper, silver, lead and zinc. To the emerging tycoon such a feat is as intoxicating as is a double envelopment to the field marshal. "One of the largest corporate transactions in history," said the *Journal*.

His hair was brown, his figure trim, his dress dapper, making him seem younger and taller than his fifty-five years and his five foot ten. He retained a kind of sinister handsomeness—eagle eyes, aquiline features, straight mouth. When he spoke, there was an enigmatic quality

enhanced by a trace of native German in his voice—a
blend of toughness and masked intentions. But, on this
triumphant morning the sharp features were wreathed in
unaccustomed warmth.

Only twenty-four hours before his bid for American
Smelting, Korholz had consummated his capture of Pan
American Sulphur, a quarter-billion-dollar complex with
$60 million in cash in its treasury. This, added to the
dominions conquered in a ten-year run of corporate takeovers—Better Industries, American Gypsum, Treesdale
Laboratories, Susquehanna, Atlantic Research, Greystone,
Xebec, Pioneer Astro, Bastian-Blessing—gave him and his
confederates sway over a virtual empire in uranium, gypsum, cosmetics, electronics, aerospace, missiles, fertilizer
plants, building materials, railroad properties, bus companies and brokerage houses, an empire of solid substances
which, he could boast to himself, had been created out of
almost nothing, out of paper, borrowed money, promises,
sleight of hand. Was anyone laughing now?

The *Journal* headlines atoned for much that had been
hard and humiliating—the long years of wandering
through blind alleys, working for minor ad agencies and
hustling for fringe businesses that, in the telltale phrases of
the dossiers, "closed down with no forwarding address," or
"discontinued" in the wake of lawsuits and creditor settlements. Even then he had the winning formula in his head;
what he lacked was access to other people's money.

In 1952, however, Korholz emerged from a series of
undistinguished soda pop and ice cream vending ventures
with $100,000—or at least the use of it. With it, he laid
claim to his first real corporate command. It was called
the Rock Wool Insulating Company, of Pueblo, Colorado.

Just how Korholz got control of it has "never been fully or satisfactorily explained" to Dun and Bradstreet. He appears to have advanced his $100,000 to one Anthony Reilly, president of Rock Wool, for stock purchases, then to have become engaged with Reilly in a six-year campaign of legal ambuscades from which Korholz emerged the survivor.

But not without suffering the sort of indignity that strews the path of the aspiring tycoon. He was adjudged the culpable officer in fraudulent evasion of Interstate Commerce Commission regulations. He was nailed by Internal Revenue for $38,774 in undeclared personal income taxes and for larger sums on his corporate returns. He was sued by stockholders for diverting corporate funds to his own use through the establishment of a dummy corporation, and for building a $100,000 house for himself at company expense (which he later bought from the company for $55,000). He was convicted and sentenced to Federal prison for unlawfully giving money to a Teamster chief. And a Federal judge found him guilty of "bad faith and malevolent posture" in a patent infringement ruse that was not without elements of drama.

Caught in the act of using the patented spinning machines and processes of a competitor, he promised to cease and desist. A year later he was caught at it again; once more he promised to desist. This time the wary patent holders arranged a tour of inspection. "Immediately prior to the inspection visits . . . ," reads the Judge's opinion, "Korholz ordered the dismantling and removal of the Downey spinners from the plant. One of the offending spinners was hid in the slag pit and the other was put in the junk pile." After the inspectors left, the spinners were dug up and reinstalled. Of such homely deeds, industrial baronies are born. It was no small achievement to have brought Rock Wool, in a few years, up to the point where it could meet a $466,374 fraud judgment.

In the triumphant years after his release from the Federal prison camp at Florence, Arizona, in 1960, Korholz had not changed his basic tactics, only the scale of his operations. The trick was to get big enough to be within the sanctuary of high corporate law; he had crossed that line when he took Susquehanna. To get there, and all the places beyond, he needed collaborators by the dozen—in corporate board rooms, in banks, among high government officials, even among friends of Presidents of the United States—collaborators who would bring him prestige and respectability along with wealth and power.

Our tale perforce centers on the grapplings of Korholz and the begrimed malefactors with whom he schemes and strains in the pit. But its portent lies equally in the immaculate accessories in the shade whose part is lesser, safer, but indispensable—those princes of the American business civilization who have raised ethical indifference to the level of a life style. Rich before a Korholz comes among them, for the sake of further enrichment such men suavely, routinely betray the very principles they are presumed to embody. On a Saturday or a Sunday in the privacy of their golf-club locker rooms, they may sneer at a Korholz—but for his uncouthness, the obviousness of his greed, never for his rapacity itself. And on Monday morning, back at the office and behind the big desk, they are once again in league with him, once again gladly selling him their principal commodity, the honor that other men bear them.

A century ago the legendary Jim Fisk, after fleeing a

maddened mob of swindled stockholders with his loot intact, had to qualify his businessman's triumph: "Nothing lost, save honor," he said. The rise of Korholz had shown that in modern America, honor is but a trapping of success. And so, on this Friday the 13th in 1968, he could enjoy without blemish the celebrity that was now his—"One of the largest corporate transactions in history."

III

At least one Susquehanna stockholder, Maurice Schy, wasn't happy with the news about the takeover of Pan Am Sulphur and the bid to merge with American Smelting. But then, Schy was an individualist. His thousand shares had jumped way up in value during the three years under Korholz, just like everyone else's—but that wasn't the point as he saw it. That was just a speculative bubble. The reality, he contended, was that the real assets of the company had been looted to build personal empires and fortunes for a few inside manipulators. The bubble would burst one day, and then the stockholders would have nothing. Schy's friends would say to him, "If you feel that way why don't you get out, sell your stock while it's way up, take your profit, and forget about it?" But to Schy that was like those "love it or leave it" stickers. No. You stay and you fight wrongdoing. You fight within the system, within the legal process, because the right and the law are on your side. Especially if you are a diligent lawyer and know how to use the tools.

Schy was in his mid-fifties, a tall, spare, silvering, attractive man with blue eyes and a voice like Henry Fonda— in fact, there was something about him of that quiet serenity and unspoiled Americana that Fonda evokes. He'd tell you he wore no halo, but you had the feeling it was because he didn't want to seem overrighteous about Susquehanna.

Anyway, back in 1965 when Korholz captured Susquehanna, Schy had started checking into Korholz, the studious way a good lawyer does, with a document to back up every assumption. And the more he had investigated the more the thing ate at him, till it grew far larger than anything that could be explained by his $10,000 investment in Susquehanna. A sensitivity to Justice is a jeopardous predilection, and Schy was in the throes of it. As Korholz mortgaged the resources of Susquehanna to add to his captures, Schy began to file suits to have stock trades set aside and restitution made. He had learned what it entailed for an individual to take on a corporation: the unevenness of the battle, the years it consumed, the dislocation of one's life, the legal costs in five or six figures—trifles to a corporation but the life blood of an individual.

He was not rich, but he had been successful enough to retire in his early fifties, to buy a condominium apartment on Miami Beach and to begin, with his wife, to indulge old loves—art, music, travel and companionship—boons too long postponed by the arduous demands of his career as counsel for the Air Line Pilots Association. Challenging Korholz had meant the end of the retirement idyll, and he had serious talks with his wife about the future. He would say later:

> This sounds so sophomoric for a man past fifty that I almost hate to admit it, but we kept getting back to President Kennedy and what he said about not asking what your country can do for you but

what you can do for your country. We took that to
heart. To get you've got to give, in any relationship.
We'd say this to each other: every time you pick up a
paper you read of terrible scandals. How long can
our society carry the weight of all this corruption?
People say, my God, why doesn't somebody *do* something? Well, *we* were somebody, so we decided to do
something.

And so he persevered. He dipped into his savings, filed
new suits and motions, went back on the road alone. Delays,
defeats and mounting costs left him undeterred. All that
was needed to remedy the wrongs in America, he insisted
with his lawyer's faith, was for the citizen to use the available means of redress and sanction. He would give the
"system" a full chance; the Securities and Exchange Commission, the Congress, the Supreme Court, whatever it took
he would do. So he had hung on, filed new actions, waited
in senators' offices, petitioned the SEC; and all the while
Korholz was scooping up new corporations and brushing
off Schy's challenge like a fly.

"We'll get our vindication in court," Schy would assure
worried friends. Maybe in 1969. Tomorrow he would
open a file on this American Smelting thing, but for now
he had something to check out on that Rock Wool merger
back in '60. . . .

IV

It was said of the original John D. Rockefeller that in his-
early years he went to bed each night tormented with
doubt that he could ever pay off all that he had borrowed,

and awoke each morning alive with schemes for borrowing more. So, too, the early Korholz, with insights beyond ordinary understanding, saw that the way to wealth lay in massive indebtedness. His prison term served, he returned to the command of Rock Wool Insulating Company in 1960 and immediately began those rapid marches and encirclements that would become his trademark. Borrowing heavily, he merged Rock Wool into Better Industries, Inc., a New England manufacturer of hair brushes and toiletries that had once enjoyed a $3-million annual business volume but had been in severe decline for several years, until its net worth had dropped to $8363. Mergers with several other impecunious firms followed, and when the dust partially cleared, Korholz and his wife and three daughters were the sole owners of a curious agglomerate.

Just what they owned was a confusing question to financial probers like Dun and Bradstreet. The mergers automatically forced an increase in Better Industries' volume of business, yet "debt in the latest statement available is many times in excess of tangible net worth . . . a description of that debt is not available." This mystery persisted for two years as Korholz maneuvered toward his next merger. Through 1960 and 1961 Dun and Bradstreet contains frequent references to Korholz's refusal to release financial statements, despite recurring promises to do so.

Indeed, concealment hovers about the man. We are not even sure of when and where he was born; the preponderance of evidence points to Rees, Germany, 1913; but he also has given out "Holland, 1903." Similarly, his academic record is only partially visible. His résumés place him variously at the London School of Economics, Cambridge University, the Sorbonne—but only for fleeting intervals that yield an impressive pedigree but no advanced degrees. He first appears in the United States in New York in 1935 at the apparent age of twenty-two, but the dossiers, for all their merciless data on closings, suits, convictions and takeovers, tell us nothing of the man's mind and its evolution.

In 1961, Korholz merged Better Industries with the American Gypsum Company, a humble maker of wallboard with sixty-six employees. Under the terms of the merger, Korholz became a major stockholder of American Gypsum and was named to its board of directors. Soon he would be the controlling voice.

Now at first look this seems a Pyrrhic progress, an advance toward ever greater insolvency. American Gypsum had lost $303,264 in 1960–61 and had liabilities of $2 million. But Korholz was not daunted by such conventionalities. Larger size, whether measured in profits or losses, can give to the gifted a greater range for maneuver, which is what Korholz continually sought. Besides, the anomalies of the Tax Code gave a perverse value to white elephants. Profit-making firms can cut their taxes magnificently by merging with big losers; they call it tax-loss-carry forward. With the merger with American Gypsum, Korholz had at last pyramided his liabilities high enough to go hunting valuable properties.

In Treesdale Laboratories, a Pennsylvania manufacturer of castings rings earning $2 million a year, Korholz found a voluptuous mate for his undernourished American Gypsum. But how does one overpower or inveigle the fair one into such a betrothal? Korholz's solution would be portentous.

He did not wage a proxy contest for control and thereby

invoke the free choice of the stockholders as to who their leaders should be. He did not bid in the open market for 51 percent of the Treesdale stock and so lay claim to rule by right of purchase. Nor did he buy a block of stock so substantial that, though less than 51 percent, it would confer preeminence. Nor could he offer himself as a genius of production or an expert in Treesdale's line of business whose skills deserved control of management. These are traditional paths to corporate chairmanships, but there is another route; stealth and diplomacy could achieve the same objective without running electoral risks or paying costs that would nullify the gains.

Suppose Korholz had his American Gypsum Company borrow enough money to buy, not 51 percent of Treesdale stock, but 20 percent. Suppose this stock was personally owned by the chairman and key directors of Treesdale and suppose he paid them an above-the-market price for it, a bonus or "premium" that meant a big profit for the sellers. And suppose, as a condition of the sale, the directors agreed to resign, to be replaced by Korholz and his men. Without having risked a stockholders election, Korholz would thus have control of Treesdale in every sense necessary to him—the power to manage, to hire and fire, to dictate the agendas of board meetings, to dominate the board and the company through his chairmanship, his control of information, his manipulative skills and the allegiance of the trusted directors he brought with him. And suppose he used this preeminence to bring off a merger of the two companies he thus controlled—fair Treesdale and spare Gypsum. Upon merger the debts of both would be assumed by the new entity, *including the debt incurred by Gypsum to buy the control stock from Treesdale's resigned directors.* Skeptics might argue that Treesdale had thus paid for its own takeover, but it was unlikely that such simplistic reasoning would find sympathy with the courts.

To bring about so bloodless a victory required a deft helper on the inside of Treesdale, a confidence-inspiring figure possessed of that background that corporation snobs call "quality." Korholz had found such a man in Edward T. Boshell. Now in his sixties, Boshell had in his prime been head of a vast utility, Standard Gas and Electric, then president of Westinghouse Air Brake. Now he was a "financial consultant"; with W. C. Fields mien and blue chip past, he moved comfortably between operators like Korholz and board room grandees. Boshell had assisted Korholz in a previous merger attempt and was again available. Korholz's banker, First National of Boston, was also banker for Treesdale and now used its influence there to have Boshell installed on the Treesdale board of directors. In due course, Boshell informed Korholz that the chairman and key directors of Treesdale would happily entertain an above-the-market offer for their stock, to be accompanied by the appropriate resignations and replacements.

The suppositions rehearsed above smoothly became realities: the purchase money was borrowed, the stock sale was concluded, the existing management resigned, the new management took over, a merger was duly effected, the purchase loan was assumed by the surviving entity, which would retain the grandiose name, "American Gypsum."

V

The union between Korholz and Treesdale was consummated in December 1964; by January 1965, Korholz was tumescent again with plans for his next liaison. The possession of Treesdale made him a more appealing suitor, giving to his agglomerate an annual profit, a look of solidity and health. He wanted a partner, as he said, "with heavy resources and widely scattered and diffuse stockholders"— that is, lots of cash and thousands of shareholders so disorganized that control could be seized by another inside deal. A series of circumstances as fickle as those which resulted in the last-minute selection of Hiroshima turned Korholz toward the Susquehanna Corporation, headquartered in Chicago. His infiltrator, Boshell, happened to be a director of Susquehanna; Boshell's son—Ed, Jr.—happened to be the Susquehanna official in charge of seeking merger prospects; and Susquehanna happened to be in the process of liquidating its major asset, the North Shore Railway, the sale of whose properties had boosted Susquehanna's liquid assets to $23 million, $12½ million of it in cash. Thus, the essential prerequisite was present—the possession by the merger victim of liquid assets greater than the cost of its takeover.

Boshell brought Korholz together with Boshell, Jr., and President Schenk of Susquehanna for preliminary talks; Korholz liked what he heard well enough to begin to set things up with his New England bankers. The battle plan, cleared in detail with the bankers, was to be a rerun of the Treesdale campaign, though the stakes were much higher. Korholz would offer key Susquehanna directors $15 a share for the stock they personally owned, which was worth $11.75; to get this personal windfall, five directors must quit the board, to be replaced by Korholz and his men. Once Korholz was in control of Susquehanna's board, the merger with Gypsum would be little more than a formality. Korholz was willing to pay up to $6.5 million in borrowed money for 430,000 shares—to assume enough resignations to give him the chairmanship.

But lowering over this golden prospect were two clouds of misgiving. The first was the reliability of the board chairman and real power at Susquehanna—J. Patrick Lannan, at fifty-nine a buccaneer of legendary machinations. The Chicago *Daily News* described Lannan as "a self-made multimillionaire with fingers in scores of corporate pies and seats on the boards of more than a dozen companies. His reputation as a man who never loses in a deal was marred just once—when his wife in 1962 won Illinois' biggest divorce settlement from him—$3 million."

Korholz had reason to know the authenticity of that reputation. A few years before, the incomparable Boshell had brought him together with Lannan in a scheme to take over NATCO, a manufacturing company with a fat treasury. Lannan held a large block of NATCO stock, and the deal was that Korholz was to purchase enough additional shares so that the two together would have working control. Boshell located a large stockholder who was willing to sell out for a price substantially above market value, and Korholz paid that price, confident that he would recoup when the takeover occurred. But Lannan had spotted a better deal and, unknown to Korholz, had sold his block, leaving Korholz holding a bag of overpriced stock that was now useless to his purpose. "God, what a fiasco," Korholz later conceded.

So he approached a new collaboration with unease. He called on Lannan to ask why he had sold him out. Lannan replied frankly, "The price was just too much to resist." For reasons that can be properly evaluated only by students of human cupidity, Korholz found this answer reassuring and happily embarked upon the new partnership. He was satisfied that Lannan wanted to get out of Susquehanna if the price was right, and he was offering Lannan a price that would mean upwards of a million and a half dollars in instant profits for him and the select group of relatives and friends admitted to the deal.

The second cloud had to do with the recent history of Susquehanna. Lannan and his fellow directors had just been re-elected after a bitter contest. To win it, they had sent proxy solicitations to the 9145 stockholders which warned that any change in management could "seriously hamper merger negotiations now in progress with several major corporations whose stocks are listed on the New York Stock Exchange." At the stockholders' meeting Lannan had given his public assurance that he would not sell his stock "even for $18 a share." Moreover, since the stockholders had been assured that mergers were being considered with companies listed on the New York Stock Exchange—an important status testifying to a degree of stability and durability—how could Susquehanna management turn around and merge with American Gypsum, a firm very definitely *not* listed on the New York Stock Exchange?

Embarrassments, yes; but not impediments. Korholz knew too well the inconstancy of corporate managements, the inattention of stockholders and the supineness of regulatory bodies to be daunted by anything said at annual meetings or written in proxy solicitations. He proceeded with his plans, borrowed $6½ million from the First National Bank of Boston, offering as his collateral the signed resignations of enough Susquehanna board members—and the designations of Korholz men to replace them

—to guarantee access to the Susquehanna millions. Explanations to the Susquehanna stockholders could be made later, when Korholz was in firm control of all the machinery.

All went like clockwork; thirty days after the Lannan group won re-election on a "don't change management now" plank, the stockholders read in the newspapers that it had abdicated and turned the chairmanship over to the stranger with the eagle eyes and the enigmatic smile.

VI

Lannan, the old manipulator, exited from Susquehanna laughing. Not only had he pocketed another fortune, he had bequeathed to Korholz an internal plague at Susquehanna that went by the name of Mike Coen. Korholz had not been the only suitor to aspire to control of the millions piling up in Suzy-Q's treasury; before his advent, Coen had accumulated control of 250,000 shares of Susquehanna stock. With it he had harassed the Lannan leadership for months and led the proxy fight that called forth from Lannan those assurances to the stockholders he so routinely discarded after election day. Coen had won only two places on Susquehanna's fifteen-man board, but in Coen's hands they represented a beachhead from which a free-swinging assault could be launched against Korholz.

Coen was a substantial foe; his early thrustings for corporate leadership were not dissimilar from Korholz's. There is a large file on Coen maintained by the National Association of Securities Dealers, an official body that works in tandem with the SEC in policing the more outrageous swindles among stockbrokers. In 1951, Coen was fined

$1000 and had his license suspended for a year for a series of shady practices that, as the judgment said, "cannot be too strongly condemned and should be severely punished." If the sentence seems anticlimactical after the findings, we must remember that businessmen trying other businessmen are like senators judging a peer, or judges giving suspended sentences to peculating D.A.'s.

Two years later the NASD condemned Coen in even stronger terms, accusing him of "multitudinous violations" and of "a display of gross disregard for high standards of commercial honor and just and equitable principles of trade." This time he was adjudged an incorrigible offender and his license was revoked altogether. Such men endure, however, and flourish in our business civilization. By the early 1960s Coen was in partnership with C. Arnholt Smith, the San Diego banker, and had won unsavory prominence as president of the Midland Securities Company of Kansas City; in the bull market of that time, Midland was underwriting many public issues on which buyers often realized a profit of 100 percent in one day.*

In 1964, Coen again achieved public notice. He and six fellow owners of Kansas City Transit, Inc., hereinafter called the "Kansas City group," were censured and restrained by the Missouri Public Service Commission for profiteering and piracy, or, in the softer words of the Commission, for "a ruthless raid on the assets of the transit company in utter disregard of its responsibility as owner of a public utility." Coen's censured partners in Kansas City Transit were pillars of the Midwest business com-

---

* Coen's license was eventually reinstated. But in 1970 protests about his activities from other Kansas City houses impelled the NASD to censure and fine Midland Securities and, in general disrepute, it closed its doors. Coen quickly popped up with a replacement.

munity; one of them, William Morriss, is now the Lieutenant Governor of Missouri; two others, A. D. Martin, a director of thirty companies, and Albert W. Thomson, once a lawyer for the SEC, now Coen's lawyer and chairman of the Board of Police Commissioners of Kansas City, were sitting on the board of Susquehanna as legatees of Coen when Korholz, flushed with victory, arrived to take command as board chairman.

Being opposed by Coen is not unlike being simultaneously set upon by Three Finger Brown and the Marx Brothers. He had made life miserable for the great Lannan by having his surrogates on the board vociferously oppose every routine measure Lannan brought up; they had even committed such heretical affronts as demanding audits of directors' expense accounts, opposing the chairman's selection of an insurance company, and voting against the pro forma complimentary resolutions without which business moguls seem unable to proceed. For Korholz, Coen had the heavy artillery waiting—a formal broadside sent to all directors by Commissioner Thomson. The letter charged that the Lannan-Korholz stock sale was a fraud on Susquehanna. It demanded that the board sue to recover for Susquehanna the "cash bonus" realized by the Lannan group, and urged the board to seek an injunction to restrain Korholz and his men from assuming office and to forbid the voting of the stock obtained in the "illegal agreement."

Korholz was wont to disdain mere annoyances, like fraud suits, subpoenas or the blatherings of the Internal Revenue Service. But like the inspired sapper who can divine the live bomb from the dud, he perceived Coen as a serious hazard that must be defused instantly. Besides, Coen gave signs of being a gentleman on the right wavelength, one he could work with profitably. Twenty-four hours after the Coen letter of accusation was distributed in Chicago, Korholz was conferring with Coen in Pueblo, Colorado.

Korholz put the question frankly, according to later testimony: "Do you want to make some money or do you just want to raise hell?"

Coen allowed as to how he was interested in making money, and Korholz said, ". . . first of all, get rid of this letter and then I will do it; we can work quietly on some program that gets you what you want as long as it is within reason and it gets me what I want for the company."

The "program" agreed upon was that Korholz would borrow more money from First National of Boston to buy Coen's 250,000 shares at the price he had given to Lannan—a $700,000 windfall for the Coen group. Coen promptly withdrew the offending letter, announcing blandly that it had been "inadvertently sent." Accompanied by Coen's man Thomson, Korholz set off for Boston to borrow the money, but this time the bankers said no. Coen unabashedly reissued his letter, which was passed out by Thomson to all his bemused fellow directors at the next Susquehanna board meeting, on June 18, 1965. Korholz temporarily buried the letter by referring it to his general counsel. Then he arranged for another confrontation with Coen in Kansas City, where he made a new proposition.

Among the Susquehanna riches that Korholz now managed was a block of 140,000 shares of Vanadium Corporation of America. Vanadium had long been anxious to buy back this block, and Susquehanna had repeatedly assured its stockholders that when it did sell it would obtain a large profit. But Korholz now offered that stock to

Coen in return for Coen's Susquehanna stock—and for calling off his dogs—a proposition that would mean a profit to the Coen group of almost the exact size envisioned in the first Korholz offer. The terms of the offer to Coen meant an actual loss of $200,000 to Susquehanna, plus a loss of the *profit* that had been predicted, and which Coen would now assay. Coen looked at Korholz and said, in that laconic phraseology that suffices for peers who are in almost wordless communion, "You're thinking along the right lines."

Korholz returned to his Susquehanna board to seek ratification of his deal with Coen. He told the board that he had offered the stock to Vanadium and that Vanadium had rejected the offer. (Both statements were later contradicted by Vanadium's board chairman, G. Lamont Weissenberger, who testified that he had never received an offer from Korholz and that if he had he would have immediately taken action on it. To which Korholz responded that, No, he hadn't personally made any offer to Vanadium, but he "thought" his banker had made a "contact" with Vanadium —a thought also contradicted by Weissenberger.

Having procured authorization from his misinformed board, Korholz introduced Coen to a power at Vanadium. Coen quickly sold Vanadium the stock just bought from Susquehanna, for $681,000 more than he had paid Susquehanna.

Korholz would later explain successfully to a judge that Coen could get a higher price because he threatened Vanadium with a take-over attempt if they didn't buy him out, something Susquehanna could not do because of restrictions arising out of previous litigation. But Weissenberger testified that he had come to terms with Coen after "simple negotiation."

Whatever the deal's effect on Susquehanna's treasury, it dramatically improved management's relations with Coen. On August 8 the sale papers were signed. On August 10, Coen formally withdrew his much traveled letter, stating as his reason that "further investigation of facts and law indicates this action is not warranted." Henceforth, Thomson and Martin would support every Korholz proposal until they resigned. And with Coen removed, only the formalities of ratification stood in the way of the merger between American Gypsum and Susquehanna. As Korholz would later say, "I was Gypsum, and I was Susquehanna."

VII

Korholz now stood at the threshold of great bonanzas. He personally owned almost 60 percent of the stock of American Gypsum and its fiscal fate was therefore inseparable from his own. As we have seen, in a merger the surviving entity assumes both the debts and the assets of both former companies. Gypsum was heavily in debt, $12.5 million of it new debt negotiated by Korholz in recent months. Fortunately, Susquehanna had just about $12.5 million in cash, another ten millions in cash equivalent, and almost no debt. Upon merger the debts of Gypsum would be assumed by the surviving entity—Susquehanna. Moreover, Susquehanna had been disposing of its railroad and other facilities, which gave it eight to ten millions in tax write-offs that would exempt Gypsum's earnings from taxation for two to three years.

Then there was the matter of the exchange ratio upon merger. According to book value, one Susquehanna share was worth four of Gypsum. But there were other ways to evaluate relative worth. If, for instance, Susquehanna were to be evaluated as a "liquidating company" while Gypsum were estimated on the basis of a going concern, that 4 to 1 spread could be drastically reduced—to 3 to 1 or 2 to 1. The more it was reduced, the more Korholz would be benefited.

Who recommends these ratios, with their power to radically diminish or enhance the holdings of thousands of absent, ignorant stockholders? We assume some impeccable personage of Solomon-like attributes—like the official New York State Handicapper at Aqueduct. Not at all. Such decisions, irrefutable and undecipherable by laymen, are made by commercial evaluating firms. No doubt many evaluators are gentlemen of dignity and rectitude; but it is a disconcerting fact that like handwriting analysts, voice identifiers, and other "expert witnesses," evaluators are wont to privately denigrate each other as "whores" and "prostitutes" when in the employ of contesting clients. Perhaps no more need be said than that the evaluating firm is often selected and paid by the successful raiding party.

The firm selected by Korholz was the New York Hanseatic Corporation. He had historical reasons for confidence in Hanseatic; he had employed them before, to set the ratios in the Treesdale merger. At that time, his chief concern was satisfying his New England lenders, whose continued backing was vital to his grandiose designs. He has testified as to why he picked Hanseatic then:

> The insurance company and the bank brought me into the Treesdale picture and then when somebody had to evaluate Treesdale and American Gypsum in a merger, we let them [Hanseatic] do it. We paid money

for this. We hired them to do an evaluation of the two companies, principally to make sure that it was satisfactory to the insurance company [State Mutual] which had a loan with warrants to buy the stock at a certain price so if the price was too low for Treesdale, the insurance companies would object *and to overcome that we took somebody that we had confidence in.* (Emphasis added.)

The Korholz family owned 1,375,000 shares of Gypsum, and almost no Susquehanna, and in the Susquehanna merger Korholz left no doubt what he wanted from Hanseatic. "I wanted the best ratio possible for American Gypsum."

He got what he wanted. Even before the merger was formally broached to the Susquehanna board, even before Hanseatic was officially retained for the job, Korholz had informed his banker of what ratio to expect—not 4 Gypsum to 1 Susquehanna, or 3 to 1, but 1.9 to 1! This ratio was later challenged in court on the ground that Hanseatic had a past relationship with Korholz in the Treesdale merger and could not therefore be considered strictly impartial, as the law required. The court found that one prior association was insufficient ground for challenge. If later transactions could have been introduced, several relationships between Korholz and Hanseatic could have been easily established. We can only guess at the total income Hanseatic received from Korholz (and his lenders) over a period of years, but every now and then a documented clue pops into the record somewhere: There was a $15,000 fee from Susquehanna for "financial purposes in connection with the merger"; a $40,000 fee for services in connection with the

Atlantic Research merger; $160,000 in retainers for continuing consultation; an option to buy 2000 shares of Susquehanna at the giveaway price of $9.25—Hanseatic exercised that option on March 6, 1968, when the market price was close to $80, making a profit of more than $100,000, and in the distance, Hanseatic would be the dealer in the fabulous $82-million purchase of Pan American Sulphur stock.

VIII

There remained only the detail of submitting the required statements to the stockholders and the SEC—they are called proxy statements—which inform the stockholders that management favors the proposed merger, describes all the good it will do for them, and purports to present all relevant facts about both companies. Since Korholz controlled both managements, had bought out all serious opposition, and had control of the official information the stockholders would receive—"the decision" of the stockholders was almost as preordained as the result of an election in the Soviet Union. Still, one must always be careful.

There was one embarrassing fact that somehow must be hidden from the Susquehanna stockholders—the $6.5-million debt American Gypsum had incurred to buy out Lannan, which was repayable by the surviving "Susquehanna Corporation" immediately after the merger. Even if such a fact were hidden in a footnote, amidst tables and graphs at the bottom of page 65 of a monstrosity so unedifying that only a few would plow through it to the end, it would have a certain sore-thumb quality that might attract troublesome notice; it would be like a man's learning on his wedding eve that his thickly veiled bride not only had no dowry, but owed vast debts that had to be paid off by him right after the marriage. And there was a greater hazard here than the threat of dampened connubial ardor. There was a law that required merged companies to maintain an unobligated cash reserve sufficient to pay off all dissatisfied stockholders who opted to turn in their stock rather than stay with the merged firm. Some clerk at the SEC might study the proxy statement all the way through and decide that cash reserves were insufficient to pay off Gypsum's debts and still have enough left over to meet this obligation. Such a determination could block the merger; the precariously balanced house of cards might come tumbling down.

Korholz talked it over with the indispensable Boshell, who had been designated to "act for" Susquehanna and protect its interests in the merger (the ironies of finance are even more delicious and sadistic than those of politics). Boshell agreed that they had "a problem of presentation." The solution, they decided, was to persuade the First National Bank of Boston to help them conceal the requirement of immediate payment. Why couldn't the records be changed to show a repayment date in the remote future—a change in writing only, of course? Korholz would make a binding oral promise of immediate repayment, but it would be a secret—from the SEC, the stockholders, even from the company auditors, to make sure they didn't enter that $6.5 million in the books as a current liability. Massachusetts Mutual and State Mutual would have to agree, too, because Gypsum owed them another $6 million, and their permission was required for any change in Gypsum's loan picture.

A more timid soul would have paled at the thought of asking a great bank and two distinguished insurance companies to participate in deception, but Korholz knew his bankers well.

The lenders swiftly agreed; but let the story be told through the memoranda of Donald Wheeler, a senior officer of Massachusetts Mutual. On September 23, 1965:

> The purpose of Mr. Boshell's visit was to indicate that for the purpose of the proxy material, they do not want to state that a condition to the merger will be that the bank loan has to be paid off. They are afraid that if this is in the proxy, it will allow minority stockholders to cause trouble by claiming that the whole deal was a scheme to bail Lannan out. . . . He is afraid that the S.E.C. could cause difficulties concerning this point as it would question whether the company had sufficient funds to pay any dissenting stockholders in the event they asked for cash.

And on October 7:

> American Gypsum and Susquehanna are now moving forward with the merger. However, they feel that potential dissenters to the merger will have a very good opportunity to take "pot shots" at American Gypsum on the basis that the merger is a "bail out" for American Gypsum inasmuch as the bank loan of $6,450,-000 must be paid off prior to December 31, 1965. For purposes of the S.E.C. and the proxy statement, the company would like to change the date when the $6,450,000 bank loan must be paid off to December 31, 1966.

And again on October 7:

> Fred Fedelli of the State Mutual called and said that
> under the circumstances, the State would go along
> with the company's request. They will accept the veral
> [sic] assurance of Bill Brown [vice-president of
> First National of Boston] that the bank loan will not
> be renewed and the verbal assurance by Mr. Korholz
> that the bank loan will be retired very shortly after
> the merger occurs.

Thus was the real repayment date expunged from the
public records, although secretly retained, and the merger
pushed through without the stockholders or the SEC being
informed of its most vital aspect.

Here, as in Treesdale and in later raids, we see the
lenders going beyond their accepted role to become the
prime catalysts in mergers, using their financial muscle to
force corporations to operate not so much in their own
interest as in that of the banks. We witness large loans
generated by piratical designs for which First National of
Boston and the insurance companies profit handsomely in
interest, commissions and the use of corporate deposits.
And the record of State Mutual reveals huge side profits
attached to loans—for the company and its key officers.
In consideration of its loans to Treesdale and American
Gypsum, State Mutual required the issuance to itself of
stock warrants entitling it to purchase 160,000 shares of
stock at sweetheart prices. For instance, one of these loan
sweeteners permitted State Mutual to buy 125,000 shares
of Gypsum stock at the fixed price of $7.00. If it went way
up, as it did, huge profits were automatic. If it fell below
$7.00, State Mutual need not buy at all. It was a risk-proof

arrangement by which they could not lose a cent and stood to make far more profit than was involved in the loan itself.

On merger day, Korholz's 1.4 million shares of American Gypsum, worth several million dollars if a buyer could be found, were automatically converted into 736,000 shares of Susquehanna that, within sixteen months, would have a market value of more than $20 million.

IX

As we watch our hero, knife in teeth, boarding Susquehanna from one side and Coen scaling up the other while Captain Lannan and his officers abandon ship, a moment's silence may be in order for the 9145 passengers entrusted to the care of these gentlemen. Who was protecting their interests? Law, ethics and custom impose that responsibility on the Susquehanna board of directors. How these directors met that responsibility tells much about the standards of corporate leadership in America, for the Susquehanna board was no aberrational collection of the shabby or obscure. Many of its names are recognized throughout the business world. We have noted Boshell's extensive corporate background, and that of A. D. Martin. Pat Lannan was a top figure of I.T. & T. and the Crowell-Collier-Macmillan publishing empire. Harold Stuart, a director of Greyhound and Skelly Oil, could say casually that among his law partners over the years, one had become Secretary of the Air Force, another Governor of Missouri, a third a federal judge, and two others United States senators, George Bard was president of Kelso-Burnett Electric. Aksel Nielsen had been head of the Federal

Reserve Board in Denver and was known among businessmen as a frequent golfing partner of President Eisenhower.
Aristocrat-banker Wheelock Whitney, a major Susquehanna stockholder and recently resigned director, was a
governor of the Investment Bankers Association of America and in 1964 had been the Republican senate candidate
against Eugene McCarthy. Arthur Wirtz was the owner
of the Chicago Blackhawks and a celebrated Illinois business power who regularly donated his Chicago stadium to
the Democratic and Republican parties for their conventions. Francis Woolard, president of Woolard & Company;
J. Earle May, of Mitchum, Jones & Templeton—these
men too had the kind of reputations stockholders feel they
can rely upon to protect and foster their interests.

At the time Korholz appeared on the scene, all fifteen
directors—except Martin and Thomson of Coen's Kansas
City group—were informed that Korholz was clandestinely
buying up large amounts of Susquehanna stock at a price
way above the market. Not only did no director see fit to
inform the general stockholders or the investing public,
but most directors traded the stock on the basis of their
inside information. Lannan and Boshell and Bogan set up
the covert change of management to be followed by
merger, but kept it secret from many of their fellow board
members and from the stockholders. Lannan, Wirtz and
three others resigned their posts of trust a month after being
duly elected and turned them over to unlikely newcomers
planning basic changes in company policy. May and Woolard did not sell their own stock, recognizing the impropriety
involved, but they used their inside information to urge the
clients of their brokerage firms to sell holdings in Susquehanna stock at the fancy price. Martin and Thompson used

their directorships to engineer the sale of Susquehanna assets
—the Vanadium stock—to their ally Coen at a fantastic
profit to Coen and a serious loss to Susquehanna. Not a
single member of the Susquehanna board took any step to
alert the stockholders to all this critical information or, except for the calculated stratagems of Martin and Thomson,
to protest the covert self-dealing taking place on all sides.

Wheelock Whitney, owner of 25,000 shares of Susquehanna, was traveling when the $15 offer was made, and
by the time he heard of it, and of the pull-out by the
Lannan group, Korholz had exhausted his credit and obtained all the resignations he needed. Did Whitney, that
elegant gentleman, protest at the traffic in stock and offices?
Not at all. He sent emissaries to Korholz to complain that
he had not been let in on the deal and to ask Korholz to
buy his 25,000 shares at the special price, even though
the offer had run out! Korholz, in his own way a statesman,
borrowed some more money and, in concert with an associate, bought Whitney's stock, at $75,000 above the market.
Wheelock Whitney is today president of the Investment
Bankers Association of America; he has taken to publicly
lamenting "a loss of values and disciplines" in the investment world, and to exhorting bankers to "self-regulation"
and "self-discipline."

Reputations notwithstanding, such men followed the lead
of a Lannan or a Korholz. Some of them Korholz brought
with him from capture to capture, nourishing them with
insider stock options or $12,000 consulting fees, confident
of their allegiance in whatever he did. Others, like the
amenable Hugh C. Michels, were given fees and favors—a
$50,000 commission on a sale of Susquehanna land, or a
steady $5000 in annual fees.

Nor did they feel that in pursuing personal advantage they were derelict as fiduciaries. Director after director would in later testimony and argument disclose a shared concept of a director's responsibilities: he joins a board primarily to exploit *his own* financial interest in the company or the interest of financial allies he represents; no matter what he said yesterday, he is honor free today to sell his stock for a bonus if he can get it and to swap directorships as part of the deal. Once he has sold his own stock, he no longer has an interest in the company that would justify his time so he may honorably quit the board even though just elected in a contest; he may even in good conscience join a company's board, not to foster that company's interests but to advance *opposed* interests, and so will consider himself "Coen's man" or "Gypsum's man" rather than the representative of all the Susquehanna stockholders. Excluding outright theft and fraud, his own personal and financial interests come before his vague fiduciary obligations to the mass of absent stockholders.

There is no cheer for the ordinary investor in this view, but it is frequently supported by the courts—as it was in the instant case where all the above directors were found to be men of "integrity and veracity who acted in good faith on the basis of informed business judgment."

If Korholz knew how to accommodate directors who did his bidding, he also knew how to backhand those who questioned him—once he no longer needed them.

"Korholz runs it with an iron hand," complained one blue-ribbon director, Woolard. "He won't listen to anybody . . . I accused him of being no good right before the board and he suggested I get off. I suggested he get off. He suggested I get off. The result is that I got off. . . . I don't know why these fellows stay on. They're all involved together."

In time, the grossness of Korholz's duplicities would arouse a few directors to their own defense, though not the corporation's. Stuart and Boshell resigned. Boshell would one day sue Korholz in a poetic falling out, and Woolard would break with him too—not for ravishing the company, but for allegedly misusing them personally on side deals. Harsh words would then be said, but when rank-and-file stockholders eventually came forward to sue Korholz in defense of the company, both Boshell and Woolard swallowed their tough talk and testified in Korholz's defense. With adversaries such as these on corporate boards, Korholz had no need of friends.

x

When the last verdict finally came down, placing the imprimatur of the Federal Judiciary on all of Korholz's manipulations in the Gypsum-Susquehanna merger, Maurice Schy could see a pattern in the untoward events that had befallen his crusade from the beginning. The difficulty he had encountered in even getting a Chicago corporation law firm to take his case tipped him off. He had gotten a few small stockholders to join him in a proposed suit, and then he had gone from one firm to another for weeks. All of them had been so enthusiastic about the case in the abstract until they learned who some of the defendants were—high-level area businessmen. Then they'd politely excuse themselves and say it was a great case but they couldn't possibly take it. The big corporations like to spread their legal work around, and their boards are all interlocked, so when it comes to a suit like Schy's the better law firms are all tied up; regular clients would be offended.

Schy's lifelong pride in his trade was dampened by this proof that the legal profession itself is often the first obstacle to justice. But he pressed on and finally obtained counsel, on the condition that he do most of the legal digging himself; otherwise the retainer would have been out of this world—for the costs would be enormous, and the chances of one of these dissenting stockholder suits winning were too slim for a law firm to gamble that kind of money on.

So the complaint was filed in Federal District Court in Chicago and assigned to Judge Abraham Lincoln Marovitz, a Daley machine product who had begun his legal career as a mouthpiece for racketeers. At the appointed time, Schy and his fellow plaintiffs assembled, their arduously prepared case ready. But before the first witness could be called, Judge Marovitz summarily threw their case out of court, ruling that the Securities Act provisions for full and fair disclosure did not apply to a "private" transaction like the Korholz-Lannan stock sale. The Schy group appealed to the Seventh Circuit Court of Appeals and that court overruled Marovitz, declaring that the law *did* apply and that the plaintiffs were entitled to a trial. Judge Marovitz would preside again, however.

"Little Abe" Marovitz is something of an enigma. One of Chicago's ruling oligarchs, quadrennially honored by being chosen to administer the inaugural oath to Mayor Daley, the judge is, unrobed, a hale fellow who is given to rendering ethnic songs in night clubs and to divulging to after-dark columnists the contents of his phone conversations with

Jimmy Durante or the trivia of his comradeships with professional ballplayers and entertainers. He is widely known for his public devotion to Abraham Lincoln; his chambers are overrun with a frightening array of paintings, photographs, busts, framed homilies and memorabilia of the Emancipator.

Withall, Marovitz is no comic figure. His background has a malodorous air about it, not unique among jurists. He first came to public notice almost fifty years ago as a bantam prize fighter on the small-club circuit. Then he reappeared as a lawyer of the political clubhouse stripe, the kind who could later be appointed an assistant prosecutor in Cook County. Then he was a lawyer for the mob, retained by such as Gus Winkler, the Capone hit man of St. Valentine's Massacre legend, and Willie Bioff, the celebrated Mafia extortionist. Finally, he was a member of the Illinois legislature.

On the bench, he had proved an industrious if sometimes erratic judge, often entrusted with complex corporate cases, and now he set aside six weeks for the Susquehanna trial. There would be no jury. The Susquehanna defendants didn't want one, and Marovitz ruled in their favor. He would decide this case all by himself. (Before the case was concluded, the U. S. Supreme Court would rule in Ross v. Bernhard that plaintiffs in stockholders' suits have a constitutional right to a jury trial, but again Marovitz would refuse to grant one.)

The pattern was set. When Schy—pursuing under court order his rights of discovery as a litigant—had found documents indicating collusion between Korholz and his bankers in hiding the $6.5-million loan from the SEC and the stockholders, Susquehanna attorneys had rushed to Judge Marovitz and got from him a court order impounding the documents and commanding Schy never to reveal them, even to the SEC, on pain of contempt of court. Now, when plaintiffs sought to introduce those documents in the trial as proof of their contention that deliberate deceit had been practiced on the stockholders, the Judge barred them as inadmissible. When the Schy group—to prove its point that Korholz had a bad reputation and that the Lannan directors were culpable for having put him in an office of trust—sought to introduce documented proof of his criminal convictions, and the tax penalties, the fraud suits, the patent infringements and so forth, Marovitz disallowed such evidence and, in a forthright and remarkable statement, showed how the court looked upon business crime:

> In this court we have men of distinction and good character who are corporate officers who come in almost every month and plead guilty to some violation, a comparable violation. I don't think it would affect their capabilities of giving to a corporation their best corporate judgment and I would not be influenced—there's no jury here—I would not be influenced in evaluating the credibility of this witness [Korholz] by this type of violation.

Then there was the element of Olsen & Johnson burlesque—the other suit against Korholz, *Mueller vs. Susquehanna,* recently concluded in the same courthouse, upstairs. Mueller was suing Korholz for the return to the company of profits he had made from trading in stock as an insider. For reasons too complicated to go into here, it was necessary upstairs for Korholz to prove that he had bought the 430,-000 shares not for himself but for American Gypsum; while downstairs it was equally essential for Korholz to prove that he had bought the 430,000 shares not for American Gypsum but for himself. Therefore, his lawyer, Attorney Rhyne, had made one opening argument upstairs and the opposite argument downstairs. Upstairs Korholz had sworn thirteen times that a certain discussion had taken place on May 1; downstairs he swore with equal vehemence that the date was May 3. Alternate diaries proving both cases had been submitted by Rhyne as evidence. And so on. Schy, feeling like the man in Kafka whose eyes were "aching from the strain of finding his way about," tried to have the Mueller testimony inserted in the record to refute what was being said in front of him, but Judge Marovitz would have none of that. What went on upstairs had nothing to do with what went on downstairs.

At the conclusion of the trial, each side submitted its proposed findings to the court. On every contested point, Judge Marovitz decided in favor of Lannan-Korholz. Of the 92 findings in the Judge's opinion, 84 were taken verbatim from Susquehanna's offering and 4 others were almost verbatim. In none of it did Judge Marovitz find any departure from normal, acceptable business practice.

In essence, the Court found that the defendants were respected businessmen of integrity and veracity acting in good faith on the basis of an informed business judgment. This is a formidable legal formula in a corporate trial which excuses much. All of the transactions described above were judged in that light. There was no conspiracy, just unconnected circumstance; no hiding of material facts, just prudent reticence; no sale of control, just an orderly change of officers in a normal way; no looting, just normal profit on a large block of stock; no dishonor in the Coen sale, just re-

moving a divisive influence for the good of the company; no
tainted prior relationship between Hanseatic and Korholz,
just a nationally respected firm doing a responsible job ob-
jectively. In none of it did Judge Marovitz find any departure from normal, acceptable business practice.

XI

Korholz was far too versatile a fellow to settle for the gigantic increase in personal wealth and corporate power which
the Gypsum-Susquehanna marriage had automatically
brought him. More was to be had, and he selected Mike
Coen as the ally to help him get it. In a rising market,
mergers invariably cause a spurt in at least one of the stocks
involved, and the man who knows ahead of others that a
merger is imminent is in a position to make hay. There
were obstacles to such personal profiteering; corporate
officers are prohibited from speculating in the stocks of
companies they control on the basis of inside knowledge
they don't make public. But there are ways and ways.
One way is to set up a dummy company to engage in
the speculations forbidden to you. Another is to find an
obscure firm somewhere, buy in low, then merge it with
your own empire, thus forcing its stock price to leap.

On September 13, 1965, shortly after the truce of mutual
profit between Korholz and Coen that cleared the way for
the Gypsum-Susquehanna merger—though the merger itself was still three months off—Coen formed the First
Greystone Corporation. Ultimately, Korholz would join its
successor, First Greystone Associates, as a limited partner.
Greystone's game was buying stock in companies that would
soon figure in Korholz mergers, and it immediately began

to buy up large blocks of American Gypsum and Susquehanna from people who did not know that a merger was
near. The price was low—$9 for Susquehanna, $6 for Gypsum—but Korholz and Coen had reason to know it would
rise when the merger plans were announced.[1]

In June 1966, Greystone again plunged, buying 80,-
000 shares at $10 a share, in a small manufacturing firm
called the Xebec Corporation. This was enough to capture control of Xebec for the Coen group. Their purpose,
according to Coen lieutenant E. F. Pitluga, was to merge
Xebec with Susquehanna at 1 to 1, or, as Pitluga put it,
"to put Xebec into Susquehanna on a share-to-share
basis." Since Susquehanna stock was selling at far higher
than Xebec, the planned merger, known only to a few
insiders, was bound to cause a big jump in Xebec stock.
Soon after Coen took over Xebec, Korholz was named to
the board along with several old regulars from the Kansas
City group. Soon, Korholz was named to Xebec's ruling
Executive Committee. In due course, Korholz proposed to
Xebec (i.e., to himself and Coen) a merger with Susquehanna without even informing his Susquehanna board.

As the price of Xebec began to rise, fueled by the
rumors and then the fact of merger, a close associate of
Korholz, one William White, was permitted to buy 6000
of Greystone's Xebec shares at a giveaway price of $13.75.
Within a month, Xebec was at $42; within three months,
at $62—representing an appreciation of almost $300,000
on a $90,000 investment.

The value of the 74,000 Xebec shares remaining with
Greystone was skyrocketing, as Korholz and Coen pre-

[1] The stock Greystone bought cost $774,004. Two years later, in Au-
gust 1967, it was sold for $2 million, a profit of $1¼ million on this
single transaction.

pared for the merger. Korholz was ready to come in now, just before the Xebec-Susquehanna merger was publicly "proposed." First Greystone Corporation sold its 74,000 shares of Xebec for $2,368,000 to First Greystone Associates, a "partnership" in which Coen and his Kansas City group were the principal partners. The profit to the original Greystone from the sale was $1,565,500—made in fifteen months on an $800,000 investment. At the merger of Xebec and Susquehanna on January 19, 1968, the 74,000 shares of Xebec became 66,600 shares of Susquehanna; within two weeks its value stood at $4,389,000—an appreciation of $2,021,000 for the brief Greystone partnership—or of $3½ million in the eighteen-month period. Officially, Korholz was a Greystone partner for only two months, for a quickie profit of $40,000. Henceforth he would join Coen in many ventures. He had reached a point where he could make millions on side deals that required little more exertion than the stroke of a pen.

XII

Side deals and foraging did not long divert Korholz from grander designs. Royally enthroned in the Susquehanna board room on Chicago's North Wacker Drive, he followed up the Gypsum-Susquehanna merger with a seven-front offensive, gradually encircling ever fatter targets. Now in control of Susquehanna's treasury, he laid siege to General Refractories, spending $10 million to corner 24 percent of its stock in late 1965. In 1966, he began his acquisition of Xebec, as we have seen, and then of Atlantic Research. In July 1968, his forces would annex Pioneer-Astro. In December of that year, Bastian-Blessing would fall captive. His plans for the seizure of the great ones, Pan American Sulphur and American Smelting and Refining, were steadily maturing.

The first to fall, the Atlantic Research Company of Alexandria, Virginia, was a diversified manufacturer in electronics, plastics, aerospace, and food-processing systems. Atlantic Research was the prime Air Force contractor for the Athena four-stage rocket vehicle system, as well as a maker of tactical missiles, bombs, incendiaries and other weaponry. Its annual revenues were running at $75 million and it was sought after as a merger partner by such estimable companies as Singer, Whittaker, and the Ogden Corporation of New York. This was stiff competition for Korholz to meet, but with his exquisite nose he smelled out the soft spot in Atlantic Research's defenses —its leadership.

Two scientist-entrepreneurs were the big stockholders and bosses. If Korholz found the chicaneries of Lannan and Coen enticing, the attraction of partnership with Dr. Arch Scurlock and Dr. Arthur Sloan must have been irresistible. The stewardship of these gentlemen had occasioned a series of tax penalties, fraud settlements and injunctions to warm the heart. An SEC finding on Scurlock and Sloan's management hummed with such phrases as "misrepresentation and fraud"; "false and misleading statements"; "failures to disclose matters of self-dealing"; "secret profits"; "mockery of the truth"; and "sham transactions designed to embellish its financial statements." That was only the beginning.

The Internal Revenue Service was about to file tax assessments of $4.2 million against the company. Scurlock was under charges of "breach of duties as a director" by his own corporation. Scurlock and Sloan had just settled four lawsuits by paying to the plaintiffs amounts of $163,000, $324,800, $260,000 and $140,000. A year before, in order to settle four stockholder suits against them alleging profiteering at corporate expense, Scurlock and Sloan had each pledged to return $500,000 to the corporation. Under such remorseless cannonading, the entire board of directors had indemnified itself, at stockholders' expense, against personal damage suits that might befall them at any moment from any direction. The legal fees for defending Scurlock, Sloan and other director-defendants amounted at one point to $908,975. Korholz surely must have been stirred to admiration by the insouciance with which Scurlock and Sloan got the company to reimburse them for the entire costs of defending their violations of the company's trust.

Moreover, Scurlock and Sloan had fallen to feuding with each other, and Scurlock was actually in the process of being forced out as a director. With the leadership divided and vulnerable to infiltration, Korholz moved in. First he approached Scurlock. Scurlock needed money, big money. (For one thing, he needed financing for the half million he had to return to his company treasury.) Korholz agreed to fix him up with a loan of $1.8 million. To arrange this opening gambit of his takeover strategy, Korholz went to a friend, C. Arnholt Smith, president of the National Bank of San Diego. Smith had several credentials for skullduggeries of this sort. He was an old confederate of Mike Coen and the Kansas City group in some of their censured activities, an important G.O.P. contributor, and a close personal friend of Richard Nixon. (Smith would be one of the select few invited to hear the

1968 election returns with the President-elect.) A *Wall Street Journal* investigative report on this self-made millionaire had labeled him a "self-dealing tycoon" who "uses publicly-owned firms to aid private ventures."

Smith, who would later join Korholz on the Susquehanna board, agreed to have his bank make the loan to Scurlock. On December 6, 1966, the loan papers were signed. On the same day, Korholz entered into the first of a series of merger pledges, first with the impecunious Scurlock, later with Sloan. These agreements were similar in that Scurlock and Sloan pledged to vote their stock in support of an Atlantic Research-Susquehanna merger; each principal gave advantageous stock options to the other and there were long-term guarantees to Scurlock and Sloan of salaries, offices and other emoluments from the new Susquehanna that would result from the merger. For instance, Sloan was guaranteed a high office with a salary of $80,000 a year for a minimum of three years. Against such offers of personal enrichment, the bona fide merger appeal of corporations like Singer and Whittaker, with their vast technical expertise, paled and Atlantic Research went over to Susquehanna.

Korholz, in the process, acquired 141,700 shares of Atlantic Research at the price of $17.50. Again, he would be in a position to profit from the inside knowledge that a merger was in the works, one that would drive up the price of Atlantic stock. Within six months this stock would appreciate by $1,750,000. Korholz was not to enjoy the fruits, however. An alert stockholder named Witofsky filed suit to recover this $1,750,000 for the company on the grounds that it was the result of insider trading. Korholz then turned the stock over to the company in pursuance of an "oral contract" he claimed was entered into before the Witofsky suit was filed. Scurlock and Sloan were not so prudent. They were sued and found liable to the company for profits arising from insider trading and were assessed heavy judgments at 6 percent interest.

Whenever corporate executives exchange such favors with each other, someone has to pay—the stockholders, the consumers, ultimately the national economy. In this case, the cost to the Susquehanna stockholders is the easiest to trace. Scurlock and Sloan insisted that the stock which they and the other Atlantic Research stockholders would receive as a result of the merger be *preferred* stock, with a par value of $5, a guaranteed annual dividend of $1 per share, and a fixed liquidating value of $32 a share, right off the top, if the company ever collapsed.

This demand created problems for Korholz. He would have to go to Susquehanna stockholders and get their approval for the creation of a privileged class of stock that would undermine their own holdings. Susquehanna had only common stock, and it had never paid a dividend. It had a par value of $1. Worse, Susquehanna had never made profits equal to the $1 per share dividend Atlantic was demanding for three million shares. Thus, under this arrangement, after the new class of preferred stockholders had received their guaranteed annual dividends, or their liquidation price, there would be nothing left over for the 9000 existing Susquehanna stockholders, either for dividends, or for liquidation if the company went bust. The Johnny-come-latelies would get it all. How do you persuade your stockholders to disenfranchise themselves?

To Korholz this was merely another "problem of presentation." On March 29, 1967, he sent out an ambiguous

proxy statement which asked for the "authorization" of a
new class of preferred stock, just in case it was ever needed,
a class for which management would set the terms. Management had no present intention to create or issue the
preferred stock, the statement went on, no plans to merge
with anyone, especially Atlantic Research. It assured stockholders that the authorization of the new preferred stock
would in no way affect the interests of the common shareholders.

Students of Korholz's past could well suspect that those
things he said he wouldn't do would immediately be done.
But such students are few, and the stock kept rising under
Korholz, so on April 21, 1967, the proxy request received
the perfunctory ratification that 99 percent of such requests
receive. Five weeks later, Korholz unabashedly made a formal proposal to merge with Atlantic Research, a deal by
which Susquehanna would issue three million shares of preferred stock and exchange it for Atlantic's common stock.
Sloan would be the board chairman of the new Susquehanna; Korholz, the president and real boss.

One more technicality remained—ratification of the
merger itself by stockholders of both companies. There
was a chance of trouble here. The evasions required for
successive victories had opened Korholz's credibility to
doubt in some quarters. The adverse suits and internal
scuffling that had raged around Sloan for years also
evoked both apprehension and a longing for decorum and
serenity.

Korholz and Sloan were enough the statesmen to realize
that a figurehead was needed, someone whose reassuring
image would lend an aura of probity and unity to what
soured minds might otherwise regard as a prospect of

mendacious and divided rule. In bygone times a United States senator or retired governor might have sufficed, but in these ungrateful days such offices inspire more suspicion than confidence. To fill the void, tycoons have developed a new institution—"friend and confidant of the President." Aksel Nielsen and C. Arnolt Smith had in the past served this purpose for Korholz and the Kansas City group, but now a fresh presidential friend was needed. Before Korholz and Sloan went before the stockholders, therefore, it was decided to bring in a nationally renowned lawyer, Charles S. Rhyne.

As past president of the American Bar Association, Rhyne stood on the top rung of his profession; as longtime chairman of the Committee for World Peace through Law, he had the patina of an international juridicist; and as a friend of Richard Nixon from law-school days at Duke— Rhyne would soon organize and run Citizens for Nixon-Agnew and would be highly touted in press speculation as a likely Supreme Court nominee when Nixon became President—Rhyne was the man to inspire confidence. Better still Rhyne was already the general counsel at Atlantic, so the principals knew his mettle. Thus it was pledged in the proxy statement that the Honorable Rhyne would come together with Korholz and Sloan in a "voting trust" that would jointly control the 712,433 shares owned by Korholz and Sloan. This seemed to mean that neither of the principals could sell their shares so long as the trust existed, thus assuring a management free of manipulation and self-dealing. It also meant that on any issue on which Sloan and Korholz disagreed, there would not be anarchy; Rhyne would cast the deciding vote and the combined stock would always be voted as a unit on any major question facing the corporation. Such an arrangement seemed to assure unity of purpose between the two chief stockholders, as well as the restraint of a prudent and prestigious hand on the reins.

The merger was ratified on November 27, 1967. The stock was exchanged and the insider fortunes were made once more. The again-reborn Susquehanna changed its headquarters to Alexandria. But the "voting trust" never materialized! Nine months later, in one of those company reports the law makes necessary from time to time, conscientious shareholders might have noticed on page 27 an admission that the voting trust had not been formally entered into. No reason was given for this dereliction; instead, it was papered over with chaff about the trust being observed in fact, though not in form. Rhyne himself, as General Counsel, was legally responsible for this statement.

Few of us would dare rely on an insurance policy that was said to exist informally though not formally entered into, even if the assurance came from a presidential confidant; but such mumbo-jumbo is often gotten by with in high finance. Regrettably, even the assurance that the voting trust was being observed informally was leaky. Other documents reveal that both Korholz and Sloan had been wheeling and dealing with the stock that was supposed to be held inviolate. At the time the statement was made, 40,000 shares had already been traded and 352,313 more were being put up for sale.

Tucked away in another company report, dated August 16, 1968, is an entry recording that Charles S. Rhyne had received an option under the Employees Option Plan to purchase 15,000 shares of Susquehanna at $41.50. We do not know the date this option was given, for it is omitted from the report—though the dates of all other options are listed and the report was prepared under Rhyne's aegis. All we know are the coincidences that Rhyne allowed his name to be used to decorate a non-existent voting trust and that he allowed himself to accept a stock option from the hands of the two officials he was presumed to be restraining in that trust, but wasn't. The option was granted sometime between February and August 1968. During that period, the stock hit $80. This represented, for Rhyne's 15,000 optioned shares, an appreciation of $577,500. Curious stockholders have been unable to get to the bottom of all this. Presidential confidants, like the gods, don't answer their mail.

The Atlantic Research coup shows us Korholz at the very peak of his entrepreneurial genius and duplicity; larger transactions lie ahead, but henceforth his labyrinthine moves are sometimes made clumsy by megalomania. Here he set up the merger, outmaneuvering the most formidable opposition and without the aid of the banks that till now were his chief resource. He did not, as heretofore, have to buy out his predecessors. Here he got them to vote their own stock for the merger, instead of Korholz having to buy it and then vote it himself. He ran no risks: The loan to Scurlock came from C. Arnolt Smith; the emoluments to Scurlock and Sloan would come out of their own company's treasury for the most part; their titles and offices cost Korholz nothing; the restraint of Rhyne proved illusory, and in that gentleman Korholz picked up a useful lawyer to defend him in the battles to come. A heavy price would be paid in the long run by the old Susquehanna shareholders, whose stock was now subordinated and whose future profits were in hock. But that was the name of the game. The ex-convict was now a partner of the United States Government in missiles, aerospace and fire bombs.

XIII

Maurice Schy had taken his lumps, financial and spiritual, and a less resolute believer in the American way would have packed it in by now. Some of his faith in the system was ebbing, but he was not yet willing to accept the view of Judge Marovitz that the Korholz approach was normal, acceptable business conduct. He followed the Atlantic Research maneuvers closely and drew up a class action representing all Susquehanna shareholders, in which he sought to upset the Atlantic Research merger by enjoining the issuance of the new preferred stock. He could not afford sufficient counsel, so he decided to help argue his own case and to take his chances on being awarded legal fees by the judge if his side won. (By the end of this court action, his bill for such costs as getting official transcripts would exceed $20,000.)

Schy vs. Susquehanna cited seven documented instances wherein the stockholders could have been misled by Korholz in his attempts to obtain approval for the issuance of preferred stock and the accompanying merger. The case was assigned to Judge J. Sam Perry, who, though not Marovitz at least, was, like Marovitz, a product of Chicago machine politics. Korholz's lawyers did not contest the accuracy of Schy's allegations. Instead, they sought dismissal on technicalities. Schy was ineligible to file a class suit, they argued, since he might be awarded legal costs and fees, which could conceivably create a conflict of interest between him and his "class." Schy waited for the Judge to laugh at the inherent spectacle involved in Susquehanna management invoking the phrase "conflict of interest" against anyone, but where great corporations are concerned the Bench is alas humorless. Instead of laughing, Judge Perry accepted Susquehanna's argument with alacrity and the case was dismissed before Schy had unzipped his valises. Moreover, Judge Perry ruled that since this was a class action, dismissal meant that no other member of the class, i.e., no other Susquehanna stockholder, could ever file a similar suit!

When the unbelievable registered, Schy pled to be allowed to step aside without prejudice to all the others. Why, he asked, should 9000 people who had nothing to do with bringing this action be disenfranchised on a technicality? But to no avail. And so a ruling that purported to protect the 9000 from some hypothetical possibility of faulty representation by Schy wound up depriving the 9000 of any representation whatever, forever.

Schy appealed; the Seventh Circuit Court upheld Perry. A petition for rehearing was denied. The Supreme Court refused to review. Period. Once more out in the street, Schy began to think about what such diverse students of our business civilization as Milton Friedman and Ralph Nader have proclaimed: In American society, the government tribunals charged with restraining business greed inevitably become the enforcers of it.

XIV

Korholz had now grown large enough to sometimes dispense with cunning; he could annex corporations by frontal assault. On July 8, 1968, along with Mike Coen and the Kansas City crowd, he bought 61 percent of the stock—absolute control—of Pioneer-Astro. Three weeks later Pioneer-Astro moved to annex Bastian-Blessing via a "tender offer"—a public offer to buy, at an above-the-market price, enough stock to gain working control (since stock ownership is scattered and divided, working control can be achieved with far less than 51 percent of all stock). The offer was successful and another corporation had suddenly fallen into Korholz's orbit.

Now for the big plunge. The plan was for a leapfrog merger with two titans. First, Susquehanna would merge with Pan American Sulphur (PASCO), and then use PASCO's assets to effect a merger with American Smelting and Refining (ASARCO). The result would be a $2-billion operation.

PASCO was a mining empire with $78 million in liquid assets, of which $60 million was in cash or cash equivalent. Korholz determined that working control of PASCO could be achieved by purchasing 38 percent of its stock. This would cost about $72 million. He set the familiar operation in motion by calling on Mr. Brown at the First National Bank of Boston, who agreed to arrange for the credit with a number of domestic and foreign banks.

The next step was to neutralize the PASCO management; if they regarded the tender offer as hostile, an attempted takeover, they would fight it and might be able to defeat it. Korholz undertook to convince them that all he had in mind was a good investment. On October 30, 1968, he paid a courtesy call on the president of PASCO, Harry Webb, to discuss a "friendly" tender offer. On November 6, he appeared before the PASCO board to allay any apprehension that he intended to raid, or loot, or take control or replace the directors. Not Herbert F. Korholz. In the tender-offer papers he filed with PASCO management and the SEC he put these assurances in writing:

> Susquehanna does not plan or propose to liquidate Pan American, to sell its assets to, or merge it with, any other person, or to make any other major change in its business or corporate structure.

Further, Korholz promised not to replace the existing board of PASCO. All he wanted, he said in writing, was to fill two present vacancies on the fourteen-man board. The PASCO management, apparently unaware of Korholz's history, accepted his words at face value and made no opposition, despite a catch-all escape hatch the wily Korholz had included thereafter:

> However, if at some subsequent time, it should appear the interests of the Pan American stockholders would be better served by any of the foregoing courses of action, Susquehanna may propose or adopt such course.

But even as he made these solemn pledges, Korholz was assuring his leaders that he would use PASCO's assets to acquire yet another corporation; he did not even wait for the tender sale to be concluded before he began proposals to merge PASCO with ASARCO. On November 7, the day after he made his promises to the PASCO board, he told Richard J. Andrews, vice-president of the Security Pacific National Bank, that the cash assets of PASCO were not available as collateral for loans because he planned to commandeer them for acquisitions. Five days later, while his bogus written promises were circulating among PASCO officials, he wrote to Andrews of his real plans:

Earnings will be substantially increased when the $60 million cash plus the ability to borrow substantial long-term money on Pan American assets is used for acquisition purposes.

The tender offer was launched on November 26 with advertisements in the *Wall Street Journal* which repeated Korholz's "no takeover" pledges. On November 27, though he as yet held no position whatever with PASCO and though the results of the tender offer would not be known for two weeks, Korholz assumed command by making an offer to the president of ASARCO to merge PASCO with it and to use PASCO's assets as security.

The tender offer turned out to be a rousing success. Korholz acquired 38 percent of PASCO's stock. So he invested another $12 million and continued to buy till he held 51 percent. At the first PASCO board meeting thereafter, the remaining Korholz promises were broken. Emissaries from the great man announced that he was taking over, after all. The board was cut from fourteen to eleven members, and enough incumbents were kicked off to make room for six Korholz men and one representative of First National of Boston. If he had lost some of his former subtlety, Korholz had raised his perfidy to new heights.

Which brings us back to that Friday in 1968 when our

story began. Korholz is awaiting the response from ASARCO. His name is this day gaudily flashing across the financial heavens like one of his Athena missiles. In a decade he has risen from unsavory obscurity to control of ten corporations and to a place among those select few whose net worth is so great it can never be accurately determined—market fluctuations may raise or lower it a million or two on any given day. Some are saying that Korholz is worth more than $50 million; his known Susquehanna holdings alone are valued at $32 million.

He lives, in these last days of the Johnson Administration, in Washington in the posh Watergate complex, not far from the White House. His incoming neighbors will be potentates in the new Nixon Administration. His employees and partners have access to the new President, clout with the regulatory agencies, influence with the courts. Prestigious associates are at work effacing the humiliations of the murky past. Charles S. Rhyne is only one. Another is former Solicitor General of the United States Philip B. Perlman, whose case is illustrative of the protective web that is so easily woven around corporate Barbarossas.

Several years before, when Korholz was awaiting sentencing after his bribery conviction, Perlman first brought to Korholz's aid the prestige he had won as chief attorney for the United States Government. The esteemed Perlman appeared before the judge in Denver to plead that the prison sentence be suspended.

"Here is the situation that confronts Your Honor," Perlman said authoritatively. "Here is a man who has not been charged before, never been convicted of any offense."

This was not the whole truth, since previous criminal convictions of firms headed by Korholz (nos. 14269 and

17128) were matters of public record; perhaps that is why this first intervention from on high did not dissuade the judge. But there would be other courtrooms in the future, and a man of Perlman's repute could be useful in embellishing history. For instance, Korholz would keep handy in the future a letter from Perlman to read aloud from the witness stand whenever some unfeeling adversary in litigation raised the question of his incarceration.

He would preface this performance by announcing that what he was about to read was from "the former Solicitor-General of the United States, Philip B. Perlman, under whom the indictment took place." Then he would read the text, which merits a place in the archives of legal sycophancy.

> Dear Mr. Korholz, [it says]
> You are continuously in my mind . . . I can't help repeating to you that you are the victim of a terrible miscarriage of justice. I believe sincerely there was no ground, legal or factual, for your indictment and conviction. The combination of circumstances which resulted in your conviction is really incredible, and I do admire you for the fortitude you are showing, and for your courage under the misfortune which has befallen you. I am hoping that experience, bad as it is, will prompt you to demonstrate that you can and will go on to even greater success not only in business but in the hearts and minds of those who have confidence in you, your ability and your integrity.

Judges would find such exhibitions convincing.

More help of this sort was on the way. By late 1968,

some of Korholz's transactions were being looked at by the Securities and Exchange Commission, and Korholz would soon hire as Susquehanna's lawyer no less than the respected Manuel Cohen, who was about to retire as Chairman of the SEC. Cohen had built up a reputation as a crusader for the public interest that should prove highly useful to Herb Korholz.

xv

It must have seemed ironic to Maurice Schy that when a court case was finally won against Susquehanna management, he didn't happen to be involved in it. Korholz, by making his bid for ASARCO and seizing control of the PASCO board, had revealed his designs earlier than was prudent. The PASCO leadership immediately filed suit to enjoin Korholz from voting the stock they claimed he had obtained by misrepresentation. And ASARCO pulled out of any merger discussions with Korholz.

This time it wasn't a case of a citizen-stockholder going against a great corporation on hostile territory. It was behemoth against behemoth, and the case was tried, not in Susquehanna's Chicago ballpark, but in the Federal District Court in Dallas, where PASCO was the home favorite. Here Korholz's use of indirection was not treated so sympathetically, and the judge found in favor of PASCO, condemning Korholz's tactics and enjoining him from voting the stock he controlled. But no hosannas, please. The legal process had not yet had full opportunity to arrive at justice. Korholz's defeat lasted only as long as it took him and Rhyne to get into the Fifth Circuit Court of Appeals in New

Orleans, where Korholz's semantical ambiguities and theory of business were better regarded. This court decided that there were ways the stockholders could have found out Korholz's true intentions no matter what the tender-offer statement said. *Caveat emptor.* The lower court was duly reversed as the legal system once more affirmed, in effect, that actions that are unspeakable affronts to personal morals are unobjectionable in corporate transactions.

In the meantime, the SEC had started an investigation. Schy had for years been trying to stimulate SEC action against Susquehanna. The stated purpose of the SEC was to protect the stockholder and the public from fraud and misrepresentation, so Schy had kept after them, officially calling to their attention innumerable irregularities. But it was like talking to The Sphinx.

For example, the disclosures provision of the Securities Act requires that if any person nominated for election as director of a publicly held corporation has been criminally convicted within the past ten years, that fact must be disclosed to the stockholders in the proxy material. This law is intended to protect stockholders by informing them about company officials with whom they are dealing.

Schy brought documents to the SEC showing that Pioneer-Astro circulated proxy statements that nominated Korholz for election to its board without disclosing his criminal conviction within the previous ten years. What would the SEC do about this violation of its own rules? The SEC responded with the evasive gobbledygook Schy had come to expect:

> The primary responsibility for adequacy and accuracy of the disclosures contained in proxy material

> including information and materiality concerning the
> background of persons nominated by management
> for election to the board of directors lies with the
> person making the solicitation.

In other words, it is the responsibility of the burglars,
not the police, to enforce the law.

But there was another way that Schy hoped the SEC
could be of help. The Commission is a repository of information that is supposed to be available to the public under
the Securities Act, the Freedom of Information Law and
other acts. Periodically, Schy would go to Washington at
his own expense, present himself at the SEC, identify
himself as a Susquehanna stockholder and a litigant, and
request information on Susquehanna that was filed with
the SEC. Invariably, the bureaucrats would frustrate his
simplest requests. One incident, trivial in itself, is significant
in its revelation of what the small stockholder can expect
from the agency ostensibly set up for his protection.

In July 1969, Schy went to Washington, to the SEC
library, to study the accumulated public record of the
SEC investigation into Susquehanna's takeover of PASCO.
For several days he sat in the library copying documents
by hand. One day he ordered Xeroxed copies of several
particularly lengthy documents that were in the public
reference room, placing his order at the desk set up for
that purpose. Presumably, nothing could have been more
routine. But ten days passed, and the documents never
came. Schy had to go back to Miami. There he called a
Miss Fulfard in the Miami office of the SEC. She said
she would make inquiry to Washington. She called back
and said she had talked to the man in charge of making

copies, a Mr. Morgan, who remembered Schy. Morgan
told her that just after Schy placed his order, a man from
the general counsel's office came down and asked what
Schy had been reading and asking for. When Morgan
told him, the man demanded that all papers Schy had
asked for be turned over to him.

On Schy's next trip to Washington he spoke to Morgan,
who confirmed Miss Fulfard's account. Then he went to
a Mr. McCoy, administrative assistant to SEC Chairman
Hamer Budge, who promised to look into it. But it was
just another charade. Ultimately, Schy got some copies of
innocuous pages he had no interest in. He never got
what he wanted and was entitled to. He began to compile
a file on his misadventures with the SEC which he entitled, "Sabotaging the Citizen."

On one of his trips to Washington in 1969, Schy heard
through the grapevine that Manuel Cohen, who had until
January of that year been chairman of the SEC, and under
whose chairmanship the SEC had begun investigating Susquehanna's activities, had just been retained as counsel
by Susquehanna. This came as a particular blow to Schy,
first because it challenged his comfortable assumption that
liberal heroes like Cohen, when it came to fraternizing
with corporations that had once been under one's official
purview, behaved differently from run-of-the-mill Republican commissioners of whom such things were routinely
expected. Worse, it augured ill for the ongoing SEC inquiry
into Susquehanna to have its former chairman, who had
for years dominated the Commission and its staff, possibly
exerting influence in Korholz's behalf.

Schy called Cohen in August 1969, and Cohen denied
any association whatever with Susquehanna. On September

23, 1969, after learning that Schy had been in touch with
the SEC on the matter, Cohen wrote to Schy confirming
their phone conversation in these words: "Neither I nor
my firm represents the Susquehanna Corporation or any
of its subsidiaries."

Nothing could be clearer or more direct; only it wasn't
the truth. For on July 3, 1969, Cohen had written to the
SEC, formally notifying them of his new affiliation with
Korholz:

> Pursuant to Rule 6B of the Securities and Ex-
> change Commission's Conduct Regulations . . . I wish
> to inform you that the firm of Wilmer, Cutler &
> Pickering, of which I am a partner, has been asked
> to consult with counsel for Susquehanna Corporation
> with reference to prospective registration statements
> for new offerings by subsidiaries of Susquehanna.
> Although I am not certain whether the firm's repre-
> sentation will involve my appearance before the
> Commission, I believe that disclosure of this informa-
> tion at this time is in accordance with the spirit of the
> Commission's rules affecting conduct of former Com-
> mission members.

And only three weeks before Cohen's unequivocal letter
to Schy, denying any association with Susquehanna, the
Senate Banking and Currency Committee, whom Schy
had alerted, had obtained a copy of an agreement made
between Cohen's firm and Susquehanna. This agreement
stated that the firm "will not represent Susquehanna in any
matters, present or future, which might come before the
SEC"—an assurance in part contradicted by Cohen's formal notice to the SEC cited above.

Only the future could reveal the ultimate nature of Cohen's new association with Korholz, but the elements of concealment surrounding its beginning were not auspicious.

On July 20, 1970, the SEC officially determined, after lengthy hearings, that Susquehanna had violated the securities laws by making false and misleading statements in connection with its takeover of PASCO. It made this ruling in the face of the Fifth Circuit Court of Appeals' decision to the contrary. For a brief moment Schy let himself believe that to a small degree the system had been vindicated, and that his conviction that justice could be obtained through the legal process had been confirmed. Then he saw that it was a victory for no one, except Korholz and the lawyers who make gigantic fees for these protracted sham battles. The penalty attached to the decision was merely that Susquehanna must amend the tender-offer papers it had filed two years before. All the consequences that flowed from the false statements—the successful stock purchase, the takeover of PASCO, the commandeering of its board and its assets—were to stand. Only a few words were to be changed, in dusty files that no longer meant anything to anyone. The decision confirmed only the impotence of the law.

When Korholz's lawyers had first brought the PASCO tender-offer papers to the SEC, a Commission official, Patrick Griffin, told them that he didn't believe the statement that Korholz had no intention of using PASCO's assets to finance further mergers. Griffin said he had been watching Korholz, and he warned the Susquehanna lawyers to reconsider their words and to ponder very carefully this time what they put in the tender-offer statement. The

lawyers said they would return to Korholz with that warning. "Korholz is the company," one of them said.

Korholz called the Commission's bluff by returning the
papers with all the dubious pledges intact. He had been
openly contemptuous of the Commission, and again was
proved right in his judgment of men and institutions.

XVI

The reckoning which had not come at the hands of corporate trustee or Federal judge or SEC commissioner came
in the marketplace. In his headlong pursuit of PASCO's
$60 million in cash, Korholz had paid no attention to
the shaky condition of its main lines of business—sulphur
mining and fertilizer production, which prudent investigation would have shown was suffering worldwide disaster.
Six months after Susquehanna borrowed $72 million to
buy PASCO stock, the value of that stock was down $30
million. By the spring of 1971, eighteen months after
that investment, the $72-million value had shrunk to $12
million, a loss of $60 million. This was borrowed money
that had been lost, money that had to be paid off. Such
losses for Susquehanna, a corporation with an earned
surplus of only $13 million at its highest, were calamitous.
The bank loan had to be met, if Korholz was ever to merge
again. So Susquehanna began stripping off its assets to
raise money. Its General Refractories stock had to be
sold, at a loss of $5 million. Then Xebec was sold at a
multimillion-dollar loss. Then Korholz announced a plan
to borrow $38 million from PASCO. But PASCO stock-
holders, still bitter over the past, fought the plan and tied

it up in a court stalemate. Meanwhile, Susquehanna stock plunged from its high of $80 in 1968 to $6 in 1970.

In mid-1971, Korholz lay in wait at his command post in Alexandria, watching for signs of new breezes. As an insider he had always stayed one jump ahead of events, always landing on his feet. He still had his dozen affiliates, his twenty-seven plant locations, and in his head the formula was still there. With certain adjustments in the game plan, new lines of credit, an improved investment climate, it was only a matter of time before . . .

Schy was back in Miami Beach, swimming in the ocean every morning before breakfast, waiting for his last appeal to come up before the Seventh Circuit Court. For what seemed an age now he had, with rare thoroughness and professional acumen, petitioned all the relevant arms of government to enforce the law. Each, in its characteristic way, had found pretexts for not acting, and the pro forma excuses they gave, piling up in Schy's desk drawers, may one day make serviceable epitaphs for a corporate machine that has thrust off the saving restraints Cardozo once hymned. In March 1971, the Supreme Court had refused to review the action by which Judge J. Sam Perry had thrown Schy out of court; the case presented no principle of sufficient importance to merit the time and attention of . . .

Schy was getting letters from senators, like the one from Senator Harrison Williams saying that his Securities Subcommittee didn't have time to hear Schy testify on stock manipulations, but if Schy would like to submit a statement for insertion into the record . . . and the letter from Senator Robert Packwood saying that he had checked out carefully the matter of Manuel Cohen representing Susquehanna and was satisfied that it was all right for a former SEC chairman to make his services available to a former litigant before the SEC as long as Cohen didn't represent them in person before the SEC, so nothing could be gained by bringing the matter before the Subcommittee . . . , etc.

Schy had spent six years, more than $30,000 in legal costs, more than $200,000 in lost income for the time he gave free to the cause. But he wasn't complaining. If he had won no salient victories, he had at least correctly prophesied a catastrophe, and that is something not given to all of us. And he had "made the record." Like Nader and Ridenhour and Fitzgerald and Ellsberg he had become part of the desperate yet hopeful phenomenon of our time: lone individuals taking up the tasks which great institutions shirk, so that we might have a diagnosis before our disease becomes terminal.

Schy is thinking he may not retire at all now. He has this idea, and he's been traveling around the country talking to law-school deans and foundation people about it, and getting a good reaction.

"Suppose," he says, "we were to set up a Small Stockholders Protective Institute that would really do the job the SEC is not doing. It could buy a share of stock in every significant corporation; that way it would get all the annual reports and proxy statements and tender-offer statements—priceless documentation. A library like that would be dynamite. Worried stockholders would be writing to us from all over, giving us leads. We could file twenty suits a year, maybe thirty. The cumulative effect would be tremendous. Why, even in losing the Lannan-Korholz case—that was *Dasho vs. Susquehanna*—the principle was established that section 14B of the Securities Act applies not just to stockbrokered sales, but to private sales among insiders—the deals among the big boys. You see, if you've been educated to look for certain clues . . ."

AUTHOR'S NOTE: On January 18, 1972, as this book was going to press, the Seventh Circuit Court of Appeals reversed the decision of Judge Marovitz in Dasho v. Susquehanna. The court found that, contrary to Marovitz, the Schy group had offered enough proof of its main allegations to be entitled to the jury trial denied them by Marovitz. Marovitz was upheld only on his dismissal of the claims against four of the thirteen defendants: Michels, who had died, and Lannan, Lauhoff and Schmick, on grounds that their resignations from the board removed them from responsibility for what was done thereafter. "As to the other defendants," the appeals verdict read, "the judgment is reversed and the case is remanded for jury trial."

The reversal was a major victory for Schy. After so many years of persevering and so many defeats, he would have his day in court, and under favorable circumstances.

The author is grateful to the publisher for interrupting the production process to include this note.

PART TWO

Controlling the Corporation

by ROBERT L. HEILBRONER

I

By a curious coincidence, I first read the chapters of this book, many of them still in rough draft, during the very week that Lieutenant Calley was found guilty of shooting twenty-two South Vietnamese civilians, and the thought that ran through my head was whether there was not an unhappy similarity between the events described in these pages and those for which that pathetic murderous young officer was tried.

For like My Lai, the incidents in this book are atrocities. Moreover, in one case as in the other, the atrocities are not merely hideous exceptions but, rather, discovered cases of a continuing pattern of misbehavior. Behind My Lai lay the unpublicized shellings of hamlets and hospitals, the "surgical" bombings from 50,000 feet, the search-and-destroy missions. Behind the incidents in this book lie the stream of petty wrongdoings over which the Better Business Bureau casts its ineffective eye, and the larger cases of more or less deliberately perpetrated harm that a careful reader can unearth, almost any day, in the back pages of *The New York Times*.

I do not wish to push the analogy too far. Yet, consider the case of Libby, McNeil & Libby, a major foodpacker that found itself hampered by the imposition of a ban on cyclamates issued by the Food and Drug Administration in 1969. Over the next sixteen months, Libby sold some 300,000 cases of cyclamate-sweetened fruit to customers in West Germany, Spain and elsewhere. "Fortunately," the *Wall Street Journal* quotes James Nadler, Libby's vice-president for international business, "the older civilizations of the world are more deliberate about judging momentary fads that are popular in the U.S. from time to time."[1] The momentary fad to which he was referring was the upshot of nineteen years of increasingly alarming laboratory findings concerning the effects of cyclamates on chick embryos—effects that produced grotesque malformations similar to those induced by thalidomide.[2]

What we have here is a business version of the principle behind the Vietnam War—the imposition of casualties on other peoples in the name of some tenet, such as freedom or profits, as the case may be. Not that Libby is the only ad-

---

[1] *The Wall Street Journal*, Feb. 11, 1971.
[2] James Turner, *The Chemical Feast* (New York, 1970), p. 12.

herent to this principle. The *Journal* article goes on to report that Parke, Davis & Co. sells its Chloromycetin to foreign nations without some of the warnings concerning dangerous side effects that it is forced to display here, and with a much wider range of recommended applications than it is allowed to mention here. The same double standard is true for Merck & Co.'s antirheumatic drug Indocin, sold abroad under much less cautious description than at home.

If these practices are not atrocities, I do not know what an atrocity is. To bring the point home, let me admit that in business, as in war, not all the atrocities are on our side. A companion article in the *Journal* tells how certain Swiss drugs banned in Sweden—Preludin, a reducing agent, and Ritalin, an antidepressant—are marketed in the United States. From the point of view of their manufacturer, Ciba-Geigy, Ltd., *we* are the Vietnamese.

Atrocities are not, of course, the only, or perhaps even the central, issue with regard to the problem of corporate responsibility. But they serve to give life to questions that otherwise tend to become too abstract to command the thoughtful attention they require.

They make us ask, for example, where responsibility begins and where it ends. Are the executives in this recital of little corporate My Lais the Lieutenant Calleys of the business world? If so, how far up the corporate ladder does moral responsibility extend? The corporate generals in this book, like those in Vietnam, are distant from the scene of the crime; and although some generals in both cases no doubt knew vaguely about "the realities," the majority almost certainly did not. It is probable that the topmost echelons of Goodrich were unaware of the faked brake tests, the board of directors of General Motors unaware of the shoddy quality of their buses, the man at the helm of the big oil companies ignorant of the bribery by their subsidiary Woodbridge—or that what they did know about these matters was very different from what we now know. Armies and corporations alike have ways of sweetening the news as it ascends the hierarchy of command. When a corporation president or a member of its board of directors says that he is "shocked" at the absence of safety devices in his plant or at some gross instance of pollution in a distant mill, the chances are that he *is* shocked, just as the Army high command was shocked at My Lai. The question is: Is being shocked good enough?

This brings us to the larger issue to which the preceding chapters have led. That issue is not merely the intensification of a search for further excesses within the business system, so that more Leutys and Sinks can be exposed. Nor is it even to devise ways of bringing generals as well as lieutenants to account. It is to ask what rules of conduct we can apply to the exercise of corporate authority from the top down, what definitions of responsibility we can impose from the bottom up.

Here is where the analogy between corporate wrongdoing and military wrongdoing finally comes to an end. For a world of difference separates the nature of military authority and responsibility from that of the corporation. Within the military world, despite squabbling among the services, a single organization of command unites the Armed Forces. By Constitutional provision, this single organization is subject to the authority of the President and the financial control of Congress. A written code of conduct, a definite system of internal justice, even an international convention, are supposed to determine the proper limits of military behavior. We all know they do not. But at least when the Army oversteps the bounds, we know where the bounds are; when it condones wrongdoing, at least we know what wrong has been done.

No such clarity of structure characterizes the system of authority in the business world. Here, for all the concentration of wealth among a few hundred giant corporations, nothing like a unity of command directs the world of business against a common enemy. On the contrary, the business world is constantly engaged in waging war against itself, as businesses vie with one another for market power. Nor is there any direct authority emanating from the central Executive or Legislative over business. Instead, a thousand laws and regulations hedge business behavior about, offering at the same time a thousand interpretations of what it can get away with. Nor, finally, is there anything resembling a system of courts-martial for business wrongdoing. The errant businessman is punished—or, rather, admonished—by society if he is caught; if he is not, he is congratulated by his fellow businessmen.[3]

But most important of all, a great divide separates the

---

[3] Sociologist E. H. Sutherland has written a famous description of the double standard of morality that protects "white collar crime." As he points out, most large businesses regularly commit numerous crimes, assuming that a crime is defined as the deliberate violation of a law. But almost no businessmen think of their activity as "criminal," although they would certainly apply that judgment to anyone who violated the law in nonbusiness areas of life. Sutherland points out that the surrounding society also does not think that business law violation is really a crime in the way that housebreaking or governmental dishonesty is. There is a difference, in the popular morality, between a businessman who may "get away with murder" and a man who really "breaks the law." See his *White Collar Crime* (New York, 1949).

definition of responsibility of the military man from that of the businessman. The general knows what he is supposed to do, and until the Vietnam War, he was rarely hard put to determine where his military mission began and ended. Moreover, until the explosion of military technology following World War II, the military man knew as well where the larger boundaries of his responsibilities ended. His purpose was to defend his country, and beyond that narrowly defined objective he neither sought nor wielded appreciable influence in other areas of life.

It is different with the businessman. He, too, is supposed to have a clear-cut mission—to make profits; and a clearly defined boundary of responsibility—to conduct a law-abiding business enterprise. As the legal profession will testify, this narrow authorization is difficult enough to de-limit—there is an immense body of law as to what a business can and cannot "legally" do in its lawful quest for profit. But beyond this ill-defined economic domain stretches the much larger and still less clear domain of the social and political responsibilities that reside in the lawful conduct of a profit-making business.

Should a business be held responsible for the social consequences of its profitable products? Are antipersonnel weapons, fast cars, electronic surveillance equipment, detergents, pesticides and the like, just "economic commodities"? Is business responsible for the human consequences of arranging work in boring and monotonous ways in order to achieve its lawful profit? Is business supposed always to support the policies of its national government by producing goods that the government orders, even if it disapproves of those policies? May business legitimately seek to alter government policies in ways that will enhance its profits?

These are questions that begin to indicate the extent and shadowiness of business responsibility—questions that put both the atrocities of the small fry and the "shock" of the higher-ups into a deeper perspective. Everyone knows that the sorts of misbehavior reported in these chapters should not be tolerated, and that the men on top ought to bear some responsibility for their subordinates. But when we ask the broader question of where the boundaries should ultimately be drawn around business power as a whole, the answers are more difficult to find. Indeed, it may be that there are no wholly satisfying answers to the larger questions. But let us defer a final judgment until we have looked more carefully into the problem.

II

It might be useful to start by getting an idea of what we mean by business power. For the conception of that power has changed remarkably over the years, and the nature of the change will help us define the problem of corporate responsibility today.

Historically, the power of big business has been identified with the power of "the Trusts," and the concern of economists, as churchwardens of the free-enterprise system, has been to warn against the consequences of trustification. Precisely what were those consequences? In part, of course, that certain corporations and their owners would make a great deal of money, John D. Rockefeller and the Standard Oil Company being the favorite examples. But beyond that was an effect that economists call a "misallocation of resources." Monopolies sell goods at higher prices than do competitive firms. Therefore, they sell fewer of those goods than they would if they were sold at competitive prices. In a word, the public is both overcharged and undersupplied when business is allowed to indulge its penchant for suppressing competition.

I would say that until fairly recently, the misallocation-of-resources argument (coupled with a considerable dislike for millionaires) provided the main thrust of the effort to control corporate behavior. Recently, however, technical studies by economists have considerably lessened fears about the degree of resource misallocation[4]—that is, such studies have shown that monopolistically produced goods would not be *that* much cheaper or produced in numbers *that* much larger if they were sold at competitive prices. Meanwhile, quite on his own, the average citizen has become far less incensed with the problem of big-business pricing than with the exactions of local labor monopolists such as the local TV repair man or the only plumber in town.

There is some reason behind this general turning away from the issue of monopolization as the single most pressing item of corporate responsibility. A few giant corporations do make giant profits—GM, for example, probably makes a pretax profit of about $2000 on each of its buses[5]; and the drug companies often make very large margins—up to 25 and 50 percent—on new prescription drugs such as MER/29. For the top 500 industrial corporations

---

[4] See "Monopoly and Resource Allocation" by Arnold Harberger, *American Economic Review* (May 1954) and "The Effect of Monopoly on Price" by David Schwartzman, *Journal of Political Economy* (August 1959).

[5] Based on an estimate of a profit of $608 per automotive unit in 1955. See Martin Shubik, *Strategy and Market Power* (New York, 1959), cited in Bruce Russett, *Economic Theories of International Politics* (Chicago, Markham, 1968), p. 158.

on *Fortune*'s famous list, however, the average percentage of profit on sales during the 1960s has been around 5 percent. This does not seem a piratical margin. Hence, with some exceptions, I think most economists would agree that monopoly as such no longer deserves the concentrated attention it once had.[6]

Indeed, looking back on the economists' obsessive concern with the economic effects of monopoly, it is remarkable how little attention was paid to the other kinds of power that very large size could bring besides the ability to squeeze extra dollars out of the consumer or to undersupply him with goods. One searches the traditional texts in vain for a discussion of whether the power of massive wealth could not be used to break a labor union or to run a company town with a heavy hand, or to finance an expensive lobby or win favors from regulatory agencies, or simply to create an impenetrable bureaucracy that would face the complaining consumer with the polite smile of the stone deaf.

If such a range of possibilities *had* been put to the churchwardens not too many years ago, there is little doubt what the next candidate for corporate responsibility would have been. This was the stubborn refusal of the big companies to deal equitably with organized labor. Second only to the complaints about price rigging, the attention of the corporate reformer of the late nineteenth century was focused on the harshness of corporate labor relations. For example, after the famous Homestead strike in the Carnegie mills (put down by the dispatch of 8000 militia), Henry Frick posted a notice reading:

[6] See, however, Gardiner C. Means, *Pricing Power and the Public Interest* (New York, 1962).

Individual applications for employment at the Homestead Steel Works will be received by the General
Superintendent either in person or by letter until 6 P.M.
Thursday, July 21, 1892. It is our desire to retain in
our service all of our old employees whose past records
are satisfactory and who did not take part in the
attempts which have been made to interfere with our
right to manage our business. Such of our old employees as do not apply by the time above named will
be considered as having no desire to re-enter our employment, and the positions which they held will be
given to other men.[7]

Having won the strike, Frick imposed a twelve-hour day
seven days per week, with a twenty-four-hour stretch
every two weeks; abolished all grievance committees; kept
all wage scales secret; eliminated extra pay for Sunday
work; forbade all workers' meetings; and cut wages far
below prestrike levels. "I would rather see the works blown
up with dynamite than turned over to those [union]
scoundrels," said Francis Lovejoy, secretary of the company, at a meeting of the Board of Directors in 1899[8]—
a position firmly maintained until the end of the 1930s. By
then, largely because of the intervention of Federal power,
the great companies caved in, and the unthinkable came
to pass in the institution of collective bargaining.

All this has such an air of historic bygones that it is difficult to believe that labor relations was once a burning
issue with respect to corporate responsibility. By this, I do
not mean to imply that the power of massed capital is no

[7] Joseph Frazier Wall, *Andrew Carnegie* (New York, 1970), p. 561.
[8] *Ibid.*, p. 632.

CONTROLLING THE CORPORATION 233

longer deployed against labor. On a smaller scale, we still find a heartless exploitation of labor in migrant farm workers' camps, where the employer is often a small-to-middling contractor who sells, however, to giant canners or packers; and to a lesser extent, labor is hard used by some big companies in the hotel and textile industries, and carelessly abused by employers in coal. Yet I doubt that most people, workers included, would maintain that *the* great problem of corporate power today lies in its mistreatment of the workingman. Labor has now built its own structures of power, particularly in those areas in which it engages in direct confrontation with big corporations; and what used to be an uneven contest of strength has now the attributes of a stand-off, or perhaps even of a coalition of forces against third parties, i.e., the consuming public.

Where, then, is the exercise of corporate power felt most keenly in our time? The two current outcries are the rape of the environment and the abuse of the consumer. That is, if you ask people: "What is bad about corporations?" the chances are the answer will have something to do with smoke or sludge, or with faulty brakes or poisonous vichyssoise.

I do not for a moment want to pooh-pooh the seriousness of both these concerns. Yet I think the problem of corporate responsibility comes into sharper focus if we look at these issues thoughtfully. The first, let us admit, is an example of "lashing out at big business" (as the conservatives like to put it) for sins that are not wholly of their making. A great deal of environmental despoliation results from our own careless behavior as consumers. More important, until very recently, the issue of ecological damage had simply not risen to public awareness, so that corporations poured their wastes into the environment with no more concern than we poured toxic fertilizers over our gardens. (In how many board rooms has the favorite aerial photo of The Works, with its great billowing stacks, been hurriedly replaced by a new ground level photo showing the factory blending into the long grass?)

Or take the hue and cry over consumer deception. Has the abuse of the buyer actually *worsened* over the last half century? I think back on Upton Sinclair's description of the meat-packing industry or on *100,000,000 Guinea Pigs,* the corporate Chamber of Horrors of my youth, and doubt it.

What, then, explains the fury with which we turn on the corporation for despoiling the air and water, and for vending shoddy or dangerous wares? I suspect that the answer lies more in our resentment of the kind of presence that the corporation represents than in the particular crimes it commits (which, I repeat, I have no wish to condone or minimize). What fuels the public protest against corporate misbehavior is the same animus that fuels the protest against the Teamsters Union or against "Welfare." It is an aspect of a widely shared frustration with respect to all bastions of power that are immense, anonymous and impregnable, and yet inextricably bound up with the industrial society that few of us wish to abandon.

This feeling of individual impotence in the face of massive organizations is by no means new. What is new is the recognition that the targets of our frustration are here to stay, immovably embedded in society. Protests against corporate misbehavior in the late nineteenth century could perhaps permit themselves the populist delusion that the offending companies—the Standard Oils and Carnegie Steels—were excrescences that could be removed from society, growths that could be cut out or at least cauterized. No such delusion is any longer possible, either with regard to labor unions, government agencies or the corporation itself. The big corporation is no longer a special case of business power and organization; it is the normal form of business power and organization. Moreover, the extent and presence of that power has been growing irresistibly. Today many corporations have incomes larger than the gross national products of some respectable nations. General Motors' annual intake, for example, exceeds the gross national product of Belgium or Switzerland; Standard Oil's (N.J.), that of Denmark; IBM's, that of Portugal. Moreover, the great companies are growing considerably faster than these nation-states. Indeed, if IBM continues its rate of growth of the last decade for another two decades, it will become the largest economic entity in the world.

Meanwhile at home the size and influence of the topmost companies expands apace. In 1968, the 100 biggest industrial firms owned roughly half the total assets of the nation's 1.5 million corporations. This was the same percentage that the biggest *200* had owned only twenty years before. All by themselves the top 10 corporations on *Fortune*'s list of the 500 largest industrials sold $100 billion worth of goods, employed 2 million people, made $5 billion in profits. Figures such as these caused the late Professor A. A. Berle to declare that we must come to think of major corporations in somewhat the same terms we have heretofore applied to nation-states.

In the face of this organizational imperative it hardly

matters whether corporations act no more carelessly than we do ourselves, or that their conduct has probably not deteriorated and may even have improved. What matters is that they have insinuated themselves more deeply into the structure of our lives and spread their influence over a far wider area of social activity than in the past. Thus when corporations rape the environment or abuse us as guinea pigs, suddenly we awaken to the realities of our individual powerlessness *and of our dependence on their smooth and presumably benign functioning.* Then our frustrations and resentments surface with a rush, in the demand that corporate power be brought to heel and that corporate officials be made accountable.

The question is How?

III

The answers to that question, as we shall see, run a wide gamut. Let us begin at the right wing of that gamut by examining the position of Milton Friedman, an internationally famous economist and proponent of what has come to be known as the libertarian philosophy:

> . . . [There] is one and only one social responsibility of business—to use its resources and engage in activities designed to increase its profits so long as it stays within the rules of the game, which is to say, engages in open and free competition, without deception and fraud . . . Few trends could so thoroughly undermine the very foundations of our free society as the acceptance by corporate officials of a social responsibility other than to make as much money for

their stockholders as possible. This is a fundamentally subversive doctrine. If businessmen do have a social responsibility other than making maximum profits for stockholders, how are they to know what it is? Can self-selected private individuals decide what the social interest is? Can they decide how great a burden they are justified in placing on themselves or their stockholders to serve that interest?[9]

In an area in which syrup flows freely, there is something astringent and bracing about Friedman's position. The social responsibility of businessmen is to make money, period. Friedman would not chide a corporation that pursued a "social" policy because it would aid its long-term search for profits, but he would deny the propriety of any activity that had no possible gain in view, even the donation of business funds to charity. Moreover, there is a clear-cut logic to his position. It is not up to the corporation to decide how much of the stockholder's money to give to charity, or which charity to give it to. Instead, the corporation should pay out *all* its earnings (instead of keeping back about half as an addition to surplus, as most companies now do), after which the stockholders should do with their money what *they* see fit, whether this be to consume it, to reinvest it, to give it to the Red Cross or to the National Rifle Association.

I am far from persuaded of the useful consequences of Friedman's view, but there is more than a grain of persuasiveness in his basic argument. When the Dow Chemical Company announces that it is making Napalm not for

[9] *Capitalism and Freedom* (Chicago, University of Chicago Press, 1962), p. 133. See also Friedman's article in *The New York Times Magazine*, September 12, 1970.

profit but for patriotism, I am sure that its directors swell
with feelings of social responsibility; and when it discon-
tinues the manufacture of Napalm in response to public
protest, I have no doubt that its officers again experience
the glow of social benefaction. But I am not sure that such
motives provide the best grounds on which social decisions
should be made. For, indeed, when Friedman asks on
what basis the businessman is qualified to make *good* social
decisions, he is asking a question that is not easy to answer.
Why should we entrust the disposition of large sums to
men whose sympathies and prejudices, not to say "philosophy," are different from mine, or from yours? How far
does the philanthropic impulse properly go? By whose say-
so are boards of directors authorized to play God?

Given the clarity of Friedman's argument, why has it
not carried the field and settled the problem of corporate
responsibility once and for all? I suspect that one very
strong reason is that businessmen themselves recoil from
the implication that they are "only" moneymakers. One of
the problems of the theology of capitalism is that capitalists
do not like to act like the creatures of pure self-interest
that they are supposed to be.

But there are other, less suppositious reasons for the
failure of the Friedman doctrine to make much headway.
One of them is that it does not squarely face up to the
consequences of its own First Rule. For if corporations in
fact sought to maximize the profits of their stockholders,
we would find General Motors lowering the price of its
cars enough to drive Chrysler and even Ford to the wall;
IBM underselling its puny competition; General Electric
driving Westinghouse out of the market. All of this would

be entirely legitimate and perfectly consistent with profit-maximizing, but it would of course be generally viewed as an exercise of supreme corporate *irresponsibility*. (One can imagine the editorials in *The New York Times* excoriating GM for using the "excuse" of profit-maximizing as an adequate explanation for driving its competition into bankruptcy.)

A second reason why Friedman's doctrine fails to convince, despite its logic, is that it makes an assumption about the relationship between business and government that is difficult to maintain. The assumption is that government makes the rules independently of business; or contrariwise, that business will acquiesce in the "rules of the game" established by government, *but will have no hand in making them*. Yet if nearly a century of regulatory history tells us anything, it is that the rules-making agencies of government are almost invariably captured by the industries which they are established to control. Thus the ICC becomes the protector and promoter of the railways; the FPC, the ally of private rather than public power; the FCC, unable to define any standard of "public interest" that might cut seriously into the profits of the broadcasting industry; the CAB, an agency whose primary aim is to limit competition among the airlines; the Pentagon, a guardian of the health of its client corporations; even the SEC, as we have seen in the case of the Susquehanna Corporation, an agency characterized by a philosophy of benign neglect. Unless Professor Friedman wishes to deny this generally established pattern of affairs, I do not see how his proposals amount to anything more than a license for business to define its "social responsibility" behind the respectable screen of a government front, after which it will indeed more or less live up to its own standards.

Lastly, Friedman's proposals rest on a curious conception of modern capitalism itself. The conception is that the rightful claimants to the huge surpluses produced by the corporate structure are its stockholders. Yet, the "ownership" exercised by the shareholder over his corporation bears little resemblance to that of the small businessman over his property. No longer even a significant source of venture capital, the stockholder is now merely a passive holder of certificates of varying degrees of risk and potential return. As to the actual operations, the available choices, even the real performance of "his" corporation, he knows little, being guided in his estimate of the corporation's activities by the collective judgment of the stock market, largely comprised of other holders as blind as himself.

That these wholly ineffectual individuals should have a "right" to the earnings of the company from which they have already been given the privilege of extracting some dividends and gambling for capital gains, seems based on a philosophy of ownership that has long since lost all accord with the facts. In the end, the profits of the corporation are extracted from the sweat of its labor force, the shrewdness and intelligence of its management, and the desires—pristine or manipulated—of the public. If any group should be given the right to determine the disposition of the corporate surplus for "social" ends, labor, management, and the public at large would seem to have a far more legitimate claim than stockholders. Moreover, since 75 percent of all corporate stock is held by the richest 2 percent of families, the view that shareowners should carry out the social responsibilities of the corporation amounts in actuality to a decision that the wealthiest group in the nation has a better claim to social wisdom than its admittedly uncertain managers—a contention that I find difficult to justify, although perhaps Professor Friedman does not.

As I noted above, few parts of the community are less comfortable with the doctrine of the morality of selfishness than the business community itself. Hence, it is hardly surprising that a quite different philosophy of social responsibility emanates from the spokesmen for the large corporation. As far back as Owen Young of General Electric in the 1920s, top businessmen have been proclaiming the need for business management to think beyond the limits of profit-making. As Frank Abrams, chairman of Standard Oil, expressed it in the 1950s, the responsibility of management is "to maintain an equitable and working balance among the claims of the various directly interested groups—stockholders, employees, customers, and the public at large."[10] In the 1960s this theme was further embroidered by Ralph Cordiner, then chairman of General Electric, with the concept of the "professional manager"—the manager trained in his task of reconciling the private interest with the public weal.[11]

Since Cordiner's company was soon thereafter involved in a particularly nasty conspiracy suit with Westinghouse (about which Cordiner declared that he himself knew nothing), and since Cordiner subsequently became closely

[10] The Editors of *Fortune*, *The Permanent Revolution* (New Jersey, 1951), p. 80.
[11] See Ralph J. Cordiner, *New Frontiers for Professional Managers* (New York, McGraw-Hill, 1956).

associated with the presidential campaign of that paragon of social responsibility Barry Goldwater, we may perhaps discount somewhat the claims of professional detachment for which he was so fervent a spokesman. Indeed, there is something hollow in the protestations of "professionalism" of a group of men who must meet no socially approved criteria for certification as managers, and who cannot be removed for failing to act in a "professional" manner.

Nonetheless, there is an element of realism in the businessman's philosophy that escapes Professor Friedman's net. It is that power is thrust irrevocably and inescapably into the hands of business management, *who must exercise it according to some criteria.* The most sophisticated expositor of this view was A. A. Berle, who described the drift of power into the hands of a small, almost invulnerable group of corporate directors, but who believed that the exercise of this power could be guided by the development of a "corporate conscience."[12]

Berle's thesis is, of course, an elitist one. Recognizing the existence of power, it entrusts its use to the largely self-directed discretion of a managerial group, rather than subjecting it to external control. Like all elitist theories, it therefore places more confidence for social progress in the benevolence of the upper classes than in the common sense of the lower.

It may be that to attain corporate responsibility we shall in fact ultimately have to depend on precisely such an internalized mechanism of authority—there have been, after all, responsible ruling groups in society as well as irresponsible ones.

[12] A. A. Berle, *The Twentieth Century Revolution* and *The American Economic Republic.*

But how responsible is the American chief executive? The question is not easy to answer. The Committee for Economic Development, one of the more forward-looking business groups, recently published a pamphlet on *Social Responsibilities of Business Corporations* that, for all its smarmy tone ("Business has carried out its basic economic responsibilities to society so well largely because of the dynamic workings of the private enterprise system"), approved a wide spectrum of forward-looking corporate social activities—aid to education, training of the disadvantaged, the support of equal opportunity, participation in urban renewal, active antipollution measures, assistance to the arts, to mention only a few.

Who could fault such a show of virtue?[13] On the other hand, Daniel Yankelovich, Inc., recently polled the executives of the *Fortune* top 500 to ascertain their views, and came up with a less reassuring picture. *Fortune* reported the results of the poll with a headline reading: "Many business leaders believe that they live in a racist society, that wealth is distributed unfairly, and that the nation needs spiritual regeneration." True enough, but *Fortune* failed to report that many more interviewees among the top 500 did *not* subscribe to these beliefs. Examples[14]:

---

[13] The answer, I am happy to report, includes two members of the CED itself, one of them an executive of the Crown Zellerbach Corporation. These heretics objected to the "carelessness of scholarship" of the report, and to its many statements that "simply do not meet any serious test of veracity." Specifically they singled out the hymns of praise that the report sang to business performance, its easy assumption of the accountability of private power, and its apotheosis of the corporate manager. It should be added, however, that the report was voted down by only three businessmen (one of whom did not state his reasons: perhaps the report went too far). Presumably the rest of the fifty-odd members lapped it up.

[14] Source: *Fortune,* October 1969.

Business is overly concerned with profits and not with public responsibilities:

	STRONGLY AGREE	PARTLY AGREE
Businessmen	5%	31%
Total Youth	51	41

Economic well-being in this country is unjustly and unfairly distributed:

	STRONGLY AGREE	PARTLY AGREE
Businessmen	6%	40%
Total Youth	31	45

Basically we are a racist nation:

	STRONGLY AGREE	PARTLY AGREE
Businessmen	15%	31%
Total Youth	28	46

I do not mean to paint the American business executive as an utter reactionary. What the poll shows me is that there does exist a minority—perhaps an influential minority—of socially "aware" businessmen; but the same poll also shows me that there exists a considerably larger majority of complacent or indifferent businessmen. This is hardly surprising—as Gunnar Myrdal has written, privileged groups in society invariably display an extraordinary selectivity with regard to what they "know" about it. Thus if the conscience of the majority of executives is to guide the future conduct of the corporation, we can predict with a high degree of certitude what course the corporation will follow. This is the course of least social change—a course that has already gashed the hull of the ship of state and that seems certain to run it on the rocks for good, if unchallenged. Left to themselves I have no doubt that business groups will address the problem of corporate responsibility with great seriousness, turning out admirable pamphlets such as that published by the Committee on

Economic Development, but leaving matters thereafter to the "dynamic workings of the private enterprise system." If we are to go beyond such pieties to actual changes in corporate behavior, something more substantial than the present state of the corporate conscience will have to provide the motivating influence.

Let me therefore deal briefly with something a great deal more substantial—the proposal that we solve the problem of corporate responsibility by the simple expedient of breaking great companies into much smaller units. Economists have long been aware that in many industries the minimum *plant size* to permit efficient operations is much smaller than the average *firm size* (most of whom operate more than one plant). Hence the suggestion to fragment large companies into plant-size companies, retaining all the efficiencies of assembly-line production, but removing the agglomeration of financial strength from which corporate power emerges.

I deal only glancingly with this proposal for two reasons. First, it is clearly beyond the limits of any realistic economic reform. It is possible that a rejuvenated antitrust movement might go so far as to split General Motors into an automobile division, a refrigerator division, a financing division etc.; or even that the core of the company might be fractured, like a mighty diamond, into a Chevrolet Corporation, a Cadillac Corporation, a Buick Corporation, an Oldsmobile Corporation, etc. But the possibility of splitting these (still immense) companies down to the size of a simple plant seems certain to encounter such a barrage of business opposition that its chances for political passage are nil.

There is a second reason why I give the idea short shrift: It is far from certain that diminishing the size of giant companies would result in a higher level of "socially responsible" behavior. Let me remind the reader of Galbraith's famous sentence in *American Capitalism:* "The showpieces [of the economy] are, with rare exceptions, the industries which are dominated by a handful of large firms. The foreign visitor, brought to the United States, . . . visits the same firms as do the attorneys of the Department of Justice in their search for monopoly."[15]

Galbraith goes on to point out that the models of powerlessness—the highly competitive textile or coal industries, for example—have also been the models of industrial backwardness, characterized by low research and development, low wages and long hours, antiunionism, company towns, etc. I see no reason to believe that an IBM cut down to size would spend its fragmented profits in a more socially beneficial manner than its master company, and I see a good many reasons to believe that such a cluster of sons of IBM might well be pressed into a competitive struggle that would reduce the price of computer service for the nation at large, but at the cost of less handsome buildings, fewer employee amenities and a more narrow view of corporate responsibility in general. The power of the corporation to work social good or evil would not be lessened by fragmenting it. It would only be made less visible and hence, in the end, less accountable or controllable than by bringing it out into the open at the top.

[15] J. K. Galbraith, *American Capitalism* (New York, Houghton Mifflin, 1956), p. 96.

Finally, let me consider still another means of coping with corporate irresponsibility. It is quite simply to nationalize the offending companies.

Back in the 1930s, nationalization was much touted as a social corrective. When the British Labor party took over after World War II, it immediately applied the remedy of nationalization to a number of key industries—coal, banking, railroads, later steel. Recently, Professor Galbraith has again raised the idea of nationalization with regard to the armaments industry, and with the advent of Amtrak—a public corporation for interurban passenger traffic—something very much like a nationalized railroad system has become a reality in America.

There is no doubt that nationalization can serve as an effective means of controlling corporate activities. The Germans have run an efficient nationalized railways system since the days of Bismarck; the French have a nationalized automobile company (Renault); the English have a first-rate national airline (BOAC); the Italians have a nationalized oil company (E.N.I.); even we Americans have a nationalized power company—the Tennessee Valley Authority. Moreover, there is no doubt that nationalization can serve at least two very important social purposes. As in post World War II England, it can provide the funds and management for failing industries and put them on an efficient footing—the British Coal Board and Railway Authority are two instances in point. Second, a single nationalized firm, coexisting with and competing against private corporations, can serve as a kind of standard bearer for the industry: Few would deny that TVA has been a pacesetter for much of the power industry.

These are by no means small achievements, and they

indicate that the nationalization of inefficient *industries* or of individual misperforming *firms* may indeed serve as a means of raising the general level of social performance. Yet, I fear that as a general prescription for assuring a high level of responsible performance, nationalization is not a cure-all. Let me cite a few instances:

Item: The same Tennessee Valley Authority that has pioneered in so many areas, is currently being sued for the devastation it has wrought in strip mining, and is regarded as a major environmental offender.

Item: In place of the wicked and inefficient private companies that once ran the transportation system in New York City, we now have the wicked and inefficient public Transit Authority.

Item: The United States Post Office, which *is* a nationalized industry, has proven so grossly inefficient that it has had to take up a new existence as a semi-autonomous "corporation."

Item: The effect of nationalizing the war contractors would be to bind in eternal wedlock what is still only a love affair between the Pentagon and, say, Lockheed Aircraft. It is the scandal of the military-industrial interlock that the big contractors are now "protected" by the Pentagon. Is it to be assumed that they will be more severely treated if and when they become part of the Pentagon?

I do not think it is necessary to belabor the obvious. The effect of nationalizing a firm is to transfer its effective "ownership"—i.e., the control over the disposition of its surplus, as well as the control over the nature of its operations—from a group of private individuals mixing their desire to make money with a confused set of social "ideals," to a group of public officials mixing their desires to make careers together with *their* confused ideas as to social ideals. Given what history has taught us about the self-protective and expansive proclivities of bureaucracies, there is no clear reason to prefer one to the other. To be sure, the motive of social service or public service is preferable to that of private profit-seeking. On the other hand, the curbs over profit-seeking—in the form of competition or of displacement by dissatisfied power groups who "raid corporations"—probably provides more active controls over the *efficiency* of private enterprise than can be exercised over public enterprise.

I do not wish to close this approach to the problem of corporate irresponsibility by writing off nationalization merely as a misguided ideal. It may be that the deficiencies of public ownership and operation are preferable to those of private enterprise. With all its faults, the TVA may be preferable to a congeries of private firms, BOAC better than Pan Am (the latter not quite an example of shining private enterprise since it depends for some 44 percent of its revenues on the Defense Department); the French or German nationalized railroads better than the American nonnationalized roads (could they be worse?). I only wish to make the point that the choice is not entirely one-sided. Nationalized corporations also pollute the environment, abuse authority, create impenetrable bureaucracies, exploit workers, defy public opinion, and generally misbehave. Shall I cite the Atomic Energy Commission's scandalous disregard of radiation hazards (plus a thick public relations cover-up) as an example? The nationalization of a failing industry, such as interurban rail service, may be a last resort (and to repeat, the nationalization of a single firm may be a bold shock measure), but it does not solve the problem of corporate responsibility. It merely makes explicit the ultimate nature of that problem, which is how to exert effective *political* control over an economic institution.

IV

It would not be surprising, considering the discouraging limitations of the proposals above, if the movement to control the corporation had by now achieved the same state of respectable crackpottery as the movement to create world government. On the contrary, the air was never more filled with plans to bring the corporation to heel.

The reason for this, I believe, lies in that general mood of mixed resentment toward, and dependence on, organized power to which we have already paid heed. Throughout the world, and in many areas beside that of business, there is visible a growing restiveness before authority, especially before unresponsive authority. The revolt against the impersonality of the bureaucracies that both support and oppress us has found its expression in sit-downs of welfare clients and in student protests against university administrators, as well as in the renewed impetus of the anticorporation movement. Moreover, the common theme that binds together these otherwise differently directed protests is their shared aim of "politicizing" the institutions they attack—that is, of piercing the aloofness of the institutional enemy and opening it to the political energies and conflicts of society.

Politicizing the corporation takes two general forms. One broad line of attack aims at making both managers and investors more *aware* of the social consequences of their actions. This strategy is typified by the efforts of the Council on Economic Priorities, headed by Alice Tepper, a former Wall Street analyst. The Council has performed prodigies of research with regard to the involvement of corporations in munitions manufacture, in pollution, in racial hiring practices and in overseas investments. It believes that the most effective weapon against corporate irresponsibility is unfaultable research—for instance, *Efficiency in Death,* the Council's book on munitions-making which described in excruciating detail the characteristics of antipersonnel and other weapons, and then the full particulars of companies involved in the manufacture of such weapons.

Another Council product was *Paper Profits,* an enormously detailed survey of paper-mill pollution, listing, company by company and plant by plant, the antipollution devices that had been installed, the amounts of money that had been spent for purification, etc. A sample of their analysis follows:

COMPANY POLLUTION OVERVIEW

Potlatch Forests, Inc. was the fourth-largest lumber producer in the United States in 1968 and in 1969 supplied 3.5% of the total plywood market in the country and 6.2% of the high-grade bleached paperboard market. A subsidiary, Northwest Paper, operates two pulp mills: one at Lewiston, Idaho, on the Washington-Idaho border, and one at Cloquet, Minnesota. A second subsidiary, Swanee Paper Corporation, operates a paper mill. The two pulp mills produce 1255 tons of pulp using 52 million gallons of water daily.

In a speech before an audience of securities analysts, Potlatch President Benton Cancell stated, "Being endowed with a wealth of natural resources, located close to manufacturing plants, our job is to fully utilize such resources." The company's pollution control record indicates that "fully utilize" is closer to "fully use up" where air and water are concerned. The Cloquet mill has only a five million gallon capacity clarifier to handle 22 million gallons of bleached calcium sulfite and Kraft effluent per day and its air pollution controls are similarly inadequate. Lewiston has no secondary treatment and its air pollution control equipment is so overloaded as to be almost useless. The mill emits over 6100 lbs. of particular matter and almost 7000 lbs. of sulfurous gases daily into the atmosphere.

Needless to say, neither mill is in compliance with state water or air pollution regulations and Lewiston is the only industrial facility in the nation to have been the subject of two separate Federal Pollution Abatement Conferences: water pollution in 1964, and air pollution in 1967. In fact, the enforcement division of the Department of the Interior Water Quality Administration is reconvening the abatement conference because there has not been satisfactory improvement in the water quality of the Snake River.

Despite the fact that there is no mention of pollution, pollution control, environment, ecology, et al., in Potlatch's annual report, the company is aware of the problem. To illustrate its concern, Potlatch ran a nationwide advertisement showing a picture of the sparkling clean Clearwater River. The text read, "It cost us a bundle, but the Clearwater still runs clear." The message was clear, but the medium was a bit muddy. The photograph was taken many miles upstream of the Lewiston mill, which doesn't even discharge into the Clearwater, but pipes its effluent to the Snake River. If the Clearwater is clean, it didn't cost Potlatch "a bundle," it cost the "price" of the Snake River and the public must pay the bill.

Not surprisingly, Potlatch ranks high in lack of cooperation with CEP [the Council on Economic Priorities]. It seems to have been waiting for CEP to go away just as it has waited for its pollution to go away. One of the company's responses to a question about air pollution equipment at Cloquet reflects its attitude: "You know, you don't just pick up this stuff off the shelf in a grocery store."[16] From the condition of its pulp mills, it is clear that Potlatch hasn't even window-shopped for pollution control equipment. Apparently production equipment is more easily obtainable, however, because the company was able to spend $27 million in 1969 on a new off-machine coater at Cloquet and a new continuous digester and bleach plant at Lewiston.

Sociology students may recall that the word "potlatch" comes from an American Indian festival during which an annual bonfire was fueled with all of one's possessions to demonstrate both wealth and the confidence of replenishing it within the next year. Potlatch

[16] Earl R. Bullock, Assistant to the President, telephone conversation with CEP, August 17, 1970.

Forests seems to feel this way about our air and water resources.

CEP estimates that, in addition to the $21.6 million which Potlatch has reportedly budgeted for pollution control at its two pulp mills, between $5.4 and $15.4 million more will be required to thoroughly clean both air and water, making a total expenditure of between $28 and $37 million.

Company Pulp Production, Water Use
and Pollution Control by Mill Location

LOCATION	PULP PROD. TON/DAY	OTHER PROD. TON/DAY	WATER USE GAL./DAY	WATER POLLUTION CONTROL			AIR POLLUTION CONTROL	
				Prim.	Sec.	Tert.	Part.	Odor
Lewiston, Idaho	830	685	30 mil.		X	X	X	X
Cloquet, Minnesota	425	330	22 mil.	X	X	X	X	X
TOTALS	1255	1015	52 mil.					

By its meticulous research, the Council hopes to accomplish two primary aims. One is to make companies themselves self-conscious about (or simply conscious of) their actions as members of a society as well as of an economy. Directors do not like to be singled out as socially irresponsible citizens any more than anyone else; and at least some kinds of practices can be lessened simply by making the generals aware of what the troops are doing. For example, when the Council's report on paper-mill pollution came out, it was roundly denounced by the paper companies, but its research findings were not challenged, and at least one company—St. Regis Paper—increased its antipollution expenditures by some $35 million.

Second, the Council on Economic Priorities (and like-minded groups) have their eye on the $26 billion of securities held by nonprofit investors—churches, universities, pension funds and the like—as well as the unknown billions held by private individuals who are sensitive to the social performance of "their" companies. (Indeed, the Council got its start when Alice Tepper was asked by a Boston synagogue to prepare a list of socially desirable investments.)[17]

What is to be expected of these investors? One aim is that they will sell the stocks of "bad" companies and buy the stocks of "good" ones, thereby exerting pressure on managers to act "better." This is a tactic for which limited hopes can be entertained at best. But the Council and similar groups also hope to motivate investors to take on the political responsibility of *voicing* their opinions with regard to corporate policy, rather than passively voting their proxies in favor of the management.

This would be, to put it mildly, a radical change in the stance of institutional investors, most of whom maintain an aloofness from corporate affairs, or simply endorse things as they are. Despite the urging of students and faculty alike, the members of the Harvard Corporation in 1971 refused to vote their shares for Campaign GM—a campaign organized to force General Motors to admit

[17] Professors Malkiel and Quandt point out in a recent issue of *The Harvard Business Review* that it would be impossible to hold a wholly guiltless portfolio—even U. S. Bonds have their socially seamy side, as long as the war absorbs so much Federal expenditure. Still, one does not have to be a purist in these matters. Honeywell Corporation, as the largest maker of antipersonnel weapons, is in a different class of guilt-edged securities than, say, Jewel Tea.

public members to its board and to form a shareholders' committee to monitor the corporation's performance. But this stand-offish position may now be changing. The trustees of Bryn Mawr supported two of three proposals in Round II of Campaign GM; stirrings on other boards of universities, church groups, pension funds, and so forth, indicate the emergence of a small but influential pressure group for corporate change; church-sponsored resolutions have already caused commotion at annual meetings of American Metal Climax, Kennecott Copper, Gulf Oil; and even Harvard has sponsored a report on its moral duties as a stockholder.

It would be asking a great deal to believe that even the vote of the Harvard Corporation would bring General Motors to its knees. But it might bring it to its senses. The total votes for Campaign GM (Round I came to only 2.7 percent of all votes cast, although it attracted almost 5 percent of all *voters*), but the publicity was enough to induce General Motors to place a Negro on its board and to establish a council on social policy. The power of social indignation, fortified by solid research, may become an influential force for making corporate management "politically" aware of the consequences of its behavior— that is, for forcing management to confront and defend, with regard to a wide range of social issues, policies that were previously acted on without reflection.

Publicity plus outrage is one strategem of the new effort toward corporate responsibility. Legal changes that will alter the actual structure or liabilities or penalties of corporations is another and potentially much more powerful

approach. Sponsored by various groups, including Ralph
Nader's Center for the Study of Responsive Law, and the
Project for Corporate Responsibility (which organized
Campaign GM), this tactic seeks the politicization of the
corporation by a redefinition of its powers and its obliga-
tions.

A full listing of the suggested legal changes would be
lengthy, but the sample below gives an idea of the spectrum
of proposals that is being advanced:

> Federal incorporation laws to avoid the present welter
> of differing state requirements and to put the corpora-
> tion (or at any rate, the large corporation) directly
> under Federal accountability.

> Greatly enlarged disclosure requirements, forcing cor-
> porations to divulge facts and figures with regard to
> antipollution expenditures, racial distribution of em-
> ployees, etc.

> Public representatives on boards of directors, chosen
> to represent various constituencies such as suppliers,
> customers, workers, or simply the public at large.

> Stiffer penalties for violation of laws that protect the
> consumer or the environment, with penalties that
> include the suspension of responsible executives.

> The required appointment of corporate officials
> charged with responsibility for assuring the compli-
> ance of their companies with existing legislation.

> Cumulative voting of shares, so that small share-
> owners, who now can cast no more than one vote for

or against *each* director, may concentrate all their voting power for or against one director.

Full availability of corporate income tax returns for public inspection.

Imposition of involuntary "social bankruptcy" for corporations that have failed consistently to abide by existing legislation.

Protection of the rights of corporate employees against corporate retaliation for public testimony with regard to acts of the corporation.

Needless to say, these proposals are anathema to the corporate world, which sees its very existence—and more than that, of course, the existence of the "free enterprise" system—imperiled by their adoption. The first round of Campaign GM was fought by General Motors as "a challenge [to] the entire system of corporate management in the United States." Is it? We can be certain that fifty years ago Mr. Roche, who is president of GM, would have been among those to maintain with equal certitude that the recognition of collective bargaining was the death blow to private enterprise. I would guess that in much less than fifty years GM will have a vice-president for environmental affairs and a vice-president for consumer relations just as it now has a vice-president for labor relations.

Indeed, with perhaps few exceptions, there seems to be little on the list of radical reforms that could not be accepted as part of corporate procedure (I must confess that I do not see how "social bankruptcy" could be effectively enforced). Many of these proposals, such as Federal incorporation laws, have long been urged, others have taken on new urgency and meaning in view of the increasing awareness of environmental damage and consumer abuse. It seems highly probable that we will move toward a considerably stricter legal framework for corporate behavior within the next decade, particularly if the accumulation of social problems turns us, at the polls, in the direction of a new New Deal.

What is perhaps a more sobering question is the difference that such laws could make. The absorption of the regulatory agencies by the corporate sector gives us good reason to regard the lasting effects of these changes as considerably less than their initial impact. Public representatives, whether from within the corporation or from outside it, will tend to be "co-opted" by the corporation, quite without any deliberate intent (not that that will be lacking), but because co-optation seems to be a law of political life. The stiffer penalties, the personal liability, the Federal law of incorporation will weed out the more outrageous cases of wrongdoing but will leave the normal run of corporate life much undisturbed, although no doubt somewhat more circumspect. Full disclosure of corporate income tax returns will constitute an additional bonanza for the public-accounting profession, which will be driven to new heights of virtuosity to convert privileges and perquisites into "costs of production" and to magnify maintenance and janitorial work into environmental triumphs.

As Ralph Nader has said: "[The corporative system] has a greater absorptive capacity than Mandarin China, and more resilience than the Vatican. Corporations, yielding when they were forced to, have in the end overwhelmed populism, organized labor, the New Deal, the regulatory state, and they will so overwhelm the consumer movement.

Any real reform will come from the disasters, not from the reforms."

Nader is undoubtedly right to apply a very large discount to the current movement for reform. Yet it would be wrong to apply a total discount. The challenges that face the corporation today are still relatively simple and clear-cut—the control over pollution, and a decent respect for the consumer. There seems no reason why these problems cannot be met by legal restrictions on corporate behavior at least as adequately as was the problem of the behavior toward labor unions in an earlier day.

Ahead lies a series of much more difficult problems, many of them not even on the agenda of the reformers, much less the corporations. There is the problem of the tedium of much work, both in the factory and in the office. There is the problem of the degradation of language and belief for which corporate advertising is so much to blame. There is the problem of the corporate role in promoting or selecting technological change itself. To these challenges, more complex and more subversive by far than those to which the current reforms are addressed, there are as yet no proposals for corporate responsibility. But their time will come, once the present problems begin to yield to the efforts that are now being mounted against them.

V

We have traveled a long distance from the small atrocities of the Lieutenant Calleys of the corporate field. Yet a nagging question remains. As we have seen, the plans for corporate reform are palliative rather than fundamental, aimed at minimal objectives and unsure even of attaining these. As Ralph Nader's statement makes clear, even the most devoted workers for corporate responsibility have a certain skepticism as to what they can accomplish.

Why, then, stop at half measures? Why not work for the abolition of the corporation—indeed, for the end of the whole system of capitalism for which the corporation is the principal agent? That question leads me to a final statement that will, I fear, be distasteful to conservative and radical alike. It is that the corporation, with its vast powers at best half controlled, is a form of social organization from which there will be no escape for many generations to follow.

The reason for this lies in the technology of our time. In all industrial societies, the provision of steel and power, computers and automobiles, even bread and water, today requires the coordination of enormous numbers of men, welded together by complex processes of extraction and assembly and transportation. From one nation to another the legal forms, the powers and immunities of the organizations that supervise this technology vary, but in all industrial societies, socialist as well as capitalist, something like the corporation dominates the economic process. That is, in all advanced societies we find semiautonomous, bureaucratic, profit-oriented (even in socialist nations) enterprises carrying out these vast technological operations—and bringing in their train an accumulation of power and influence that eludes effective control.

That is not, however, the full extent of the dilemma of our age. A more terrible fact is that we do not know any better way to organize mankind in the immense numbers needed to operate our technology, other than by utilizing the motives of acquisitiveness or bureaucratic conformity through which the corporation exerts its dominion over men. In small-scale communities, men cooperate. But men can no longer live in small communities on this crowded planet, even if they wanted to. In large communities, men contend; and some means must be found to concert their energies to the common needs of survival.

Nothing is more sobering in this regard than that socialism—the hope of the future and the despair of the present—must use as its main weapon against the irrationalities of corporate capitalism the irrationalities of the nation-state, and that all its efforts to bind together a large society by appeals other than to man's acquisitiveness or to his patriotism have proved delusive.[18]

I do not know which institution it is more blasphemous to

[18] I think I should add a longish footnote here. First, there is the question of whether the commune movement which has sprung up among our youth does not represent a way out of this dilemma. For a few perhaps it does. Communes may represent a useful sanctuary for some, but they are essentially a parasitic form of social organization, not a harbinger of a new form.

Much more important is another mode of social organization, represented today mainly by Yugoslavia. This is the worker-managed economy, where workers exercise the supervisory powers now delegated to boards of directors, and thereby participate in the decision-making that affects their economic lives. Worker-managed enterprises are often said to present the most practical alternative to bureaucratic and hierarchical enterprise. The reason that I consign this hopeful thought to a footnote is that I am far from convinced that worker management will succeed in practice to the extent that its fervent well-wishers hope. I am impressed by an argument posed by political scientist Robert Dahl in his brilliant *After the Revolution?* Workers do not *want* to participate in the operation of "their" enterprises, says Dahl. What workers seek is not more involvement with the factory, but less. They want high pay, short hours and good working conditions from their jobs; but their participatory energies are reserved for their families, their local interests, their outside political affiliations.

There is a ring of chastening truth in Dahl's contentions. But I would not want to write the worker-managed enterprise off until it had been given a full try. It is unfortunate that Yugoslavia, with its regional divisions and disadvantaged economic status, must be the testing ground for a social experiment of great potential value for the industrialized world.

challenge—the nation-state with its flags and parades, its solemn mystical unity, and its latent ferocity; or the corporation with its insatiable wealth-seeking, its dehumanizing calculus of plus and minus, its careful inculcation of impulses and goals that should at most be tolerated. Nevertheless, I write these dangerous words to put the problem of this book in proper focus. We are easily misled by the gleaming technology of our age into thinking that we live at a time when men are also highly polished, or would be if only the present institutions were changed for other ones. We might as well believe that the shining armor of the knight encased a person of superior morality as well as strength. Capitalism and nationalism—the driving forces of our time—persist by their capacity to appeal to that which is as primitive as it is powerful. I do not say that men cannot become more socialized, or that a world without corporations, without nationalism, may not be the destination toward which we are gradually making our way. But as things now stand, the corporation that binds men together by appealing to their acquisitive natures, and the state that binds them together by appealing to their patriotic natures, are the only means we have for ensuring our survival, even if by a terrible irony they are also the institutions by which our survival is most seriously endangered.

So we shall have to live with the corporation as we shall have to live with the nation-state. Indeed the prospect is that the corporation and the nation-state will become more closely knit under plannified capitalism—motives of patriotism infusing the key firms in the private sector; the calculus of economic benefit (suitably amended to represent the "public interest") informing the public sector.

Does this render futile all efforts to achieve corporate

responsibility? On the contrary, the very persistence of the corporation gives to the search for responsibility a deeper significance than the remedy of the abuses of the moment. The creation of a responsive and responsible corporation becomes an indispensable step in the creation of a responsive and responsible state—perhaps the central social problem of our age. If this chapter has made it clear that achieving this goal is much more complex than we tend to imagine, this is only because the task of humanizing all social organizations is a profoundly difficult one. I do not wish to dishearten the crusader for corporate responsibility. May his cause prevail. But little is gained when we delude ourselves as to the ease with which human society can be restructured. The cause of reform, not to mention that of constructive revolution, is too important to be nurtured on anything but the truth.

INDEX

272

INDEX